SELLING AMONG
WOLVES

Michael Q. Pink

SELLING AMONG WOLVES

WITHOUT JOINING THE PACK!

Bridge-Logos

Gainesville, Florida 32614 USA

SELLING AMONG WOLVES

Michael Q. Pink

"Behold, I send you forth as sheep in the midst of wolves, Be ye therefore wise as serpents and harmless as doves."

Jesus Christ

Bridge-Logos
Gainesville, Florida 32614 USA

Printed in the United States of America.

04 00   2   1

Library of Congress Catalog Card Number: 00-105356

International Standard Book Number: 0-88270-826-0

Contents

In Honor of
The Greatest Salesman
of the 20th Century

Growing up, my father cautioned me against a career in sales. He spent most of his adult life excelling in sales with different companies like Brunswick of Canada. He knew the games that were played and the wolves that played them. He'd been bitten a few times, but never succumbed to their ways. He saw my naiveté and warned they would try to eat me alive. To survive among wolves, he cautioned, many simply join the pack and become wolves, and he didn't want that for me.

He had fought his battles in WWII, and fighting the wolves in the marketplace was just another battle for him. But he knew I had no battle experience, and he worried about me going into the marketplace unprepared for the hungry wolves I would have to compete with. He underestimated the example he had set before me of honesty and integrity, generosity and love, grit and courage.

Quite unintentionally, a few years later I found myself on the same path he had walked so long ago, and I quickly learned that the values he had imparted to me by example had taken root. I was more of a "chip off the old block" than either of us ever anticipated. In the years that have followed I have written or co-written a dozen other books, but I always knew that when I wrote a book on selling, I would dedicate it to him. I only wish he could have lived to see the day and to know how much I admire him.

Peter Pink

1916– 1996

First Word

I wrote this book for one reason. It needed to be written. There are lots of books on sales. Some good, some bad. But on what authority do they base their knowledge? For most, it's based upon personal experience and I can learn from their experience. For some it's based upon research of thousands of other salespeople. (They themselves having never had the courage, calling or confidence to enter the fray.) It's similar to taking advice from a man who has studied war, but never fought in one. I can learn from him also, but I would rather learn from One who was there, who fought and who won. I've found such a One. He wrote the book on business and life. He's intimately familiar with war and peace and He holds all things together by the word of His power. Do you really think it's a stretch for Him to understand the selling process? I don't think so.

We all have a grid through which we interpret life. It's our world view and it's how we filter the information coming to us. Do you know the worldview of those who have influenced your thinking on sales? Does it matter to you? It matters to me. Some say that truth is truth no matter where you learn it, but it's the spin on the truth that concerns me. And truth separated from the Giver of Truth, is like a bottle of cool water in a dry place. It's very refreshing, but unless you know where to get some more of that water, you will slowly die of thirst. And if that truth is mixed with a little poison, it may hasten the effect.

Generally speaking, corporate America doesn't welcome spiritual truth in their hallowed boardrooms. They have shunned the pristine streams of God's ever flowing Truth in exchange for the polluted, stagnant mixture of truth and error, drawn from the bitter wells of self-promoting, motivational gurus. Haggai, the fiery Old Testament prophet, reminds us that when the unclean mixes with the clean, they both become unclean. Jesus said it simply; "a little leaven, leavens the whole."

This book is about approaching the selling process from a biblical perspective. It's about adapting biblical models of conquest and service, to the marketplace. Others have chosen role models ranging from Sun Tzu to Attila the Hun and adapted their practices to the selling process. It can be done, but there is a better way.

It's time to move beyond veiled references to some "higher power" and rip off the veil of political correctness with which we cover the Truth, and let it shine for all to see. God didn't light a candle in us to hide it under a bushel. In fact, He told us "Let your light so shine before men, that they may see your good works and glorify your Father in Heaven." Let's use the light God gave us to find the path, walk in it and lead others to it. Let's go out into the marketplace and excel without compromising our values. This book removes the veil and in a clear and compelling manner shows any who are willing to see, biblical principles and strategies for succeeding in a highly competitive sales environment.

It's an honest attempt to both serve you bottles of cool water, while simultaneously pointing you to the River so you'll never have to search for water again. You might have to work up a sweat drawing the water out of the River, but you'll never have to look for the River again. There are a lot of wonderful folks living by the river that have been bottling the water and selling it in the marketplace for years. I'm tired of bottled water and I don't want to sell you any either. I want to take you to the River so you can drink and never run dry. Want to come?

Systems in Conflict

Most of us are called into the world of commerce. It's our mission field, our livelihood, and it's full of risk, noise and potential reward. In many respects, this world of commerce is like a huge sawmill that is operated by a pack of wolves. The workforce is a combination of sheep and wolves, and some of the wolves wear sheep's clothing and some of the sheep wear wolves' clothing. Not only is it a confusing world, but it is also hard to know which individuals are trustworthy and which aren't.

When I first entered that world as a sheep, I was trained in the ways of the wolf with promises that if I went along with their system, I would go far. But nobody told me it was the way of the wolf; I was just told it was the way things were done. The system or "way of doing things" appears to have little resistance. It's the status quo. To find a way contrary to the status quo and then to attempt to operate within the system is not for the faint of heart. The status quo is like a buzz saw with a roar that is never far away, and the floor is littered with the body parts of those who either ignored the buzz saw or were ignorant of how it really worked.

In this wolf-like world of "go with the system or else," consider the Lamb of God. He's partial to working with wood, He's a carpenter, and His Dad owns the sawmill. He was aware of the way things were handled in the sawmill and He not only claimed there was a better way, but He insisted that He Himself was the Way. The common people, some of whom had lost limbs to the system, put their hope in Him. Could it be that Jesus Christ really was the Son of the Owner? Could it be that He really did have a better way? Can we trust Him? Would we really be better off? What if the wolves found out that we were still working in the sawmill but no longer accepted their leadership? How would they react?

Predictably, too much was at stake. They had no choice but to kill the Owner's Son, so they nailed him to a piece of timber and fed Him through the buzz saw. When He cried out, "It is finished!" everyone wondered what He meant. No one had ever survived the buzz saw before, but three days later He showed up at the sawmill alive—in one piece—and very much in charge! It was obvious that He had all power and authority. He said He wanted us to tell others about His Way, then added that the Owner had plans to expand the sawmill and that His plans would prevail.

Two thousand years later, the sawmill of commerce is still full of sheep and wolves, each vying for key leadership roles to set policy, establish procedures and distribute profits. The Owner chose to accomplish His agenda largely through us, the workers, but many abdicated their responsibility and let the wolves run the mill. As a result, the quality has gone down, fewer profits find their way to the Owner and the healthy sheep look more and more like wolves while the weaker sheep live in fear. It seems their only hope is that the Owner's Son will come back again and set things permanently in order, but while they wait, the sawmill deteriorates. And this does not please the Owner, nor does it enhance His reputation on Earth. However, He is doing something about it! He's calling you and me to follow His example of leading through service, and in so doing, we regain the portals of power and His name is glorified.

Frank Lyman, a business associate, once said, "The Christian life is a vicarious life. It is Christ living through us to accomplish His will on Earth. We are His hands to feed the hungry and clothe the naked. We are His voice to heal the broken-hearted and comfort the afflicted." We are also His representatives at the sawmill to raise a righteous standard and create the environment where His work can carry on undeterred. However, at the corporate, policy-setting level of the sawmill, our voice has for the most part fallen silent.

When we first enter the world of commerce, we are told how to conform and are then expected to do so. When I began my career in sales, I had no idea there were two systems based on two very different worldviews with two entirely different outcomes. I understood my mission was to work in the sawmill so I could fund the work of the Kingdom. If possible, I was to very discreetly share the gospel with co-workers and lead them to Christ. No one told me that we could be a lot more effective at this if we ran the sawmill!

It's understood that we are to submit to the tyranny without succumbing to its values. So I entered the world of sales much like many of you did, through what Dennis Peacock calls, Pharaoh's School. It was there that they taught me the ways of Egypt (the ways of the flesh or carnal nature). I wanted to learn God's Way, but instead I was taught by reputable companies the subtle ways to appeal to a person's pride, greed, or love of whatever the world had to offer. In short, I was taught how to appeal to the very side of human nature I thought I was called to disdain.

In the years that followed, I struggled to find the Father's Way for succeeding in sales. I knew I was called to the business arena and I could see the fundamental flaws of the established system of selling. I had learned twenty ways to close a sale, but what I really needed was one good way to open a relationship. I'd been taught how to create artificial need, but what I needed to know was how to simply uncover the genuine need that already existed and meet it. Instead of finding ample Biblical resources to help me, all I could find were a few Egyptian versions with Bible verses taped on them. They looked good, but the results were about the same.

Then one day it all changed. I had taken a job selling copiers in a new city, and though I knew for sure that I didn't want to sell copiers, it seemed that God had opened up the job for me. On the first day, the vice-president of sales told me his expectations: "We don't expect you to sell anything your first month, but we expect you to sell two copiers your second month and four copiers per month thereafter." What he didn't tell me was that no new sales reps had ever made six sales in their first ninety days. He went on to explain, "We expect you to sell one out of four or one out of five demonstrations that you do. The national average is one out of four."

When I went home from work that day, my wife could see that I was upset and asked what was bothering me. I told her, "They said I need to sell one out of four copiers that I demonstrate." She didn't see what was wrong with that. I explained that it meant I was supposed to accept a seventy-five percent failure rate, and I wasn't happy about that.

I reasoned, "What farmer plants four rows of corn and then prays to God that just one of them will come up?" I picked up my Bible and told her that I didn't really want to sell copiers, but it seemed that God had me there, so I was going to study His Word to find principles and strategies that I could apply to sales. If the Father really had a better way, I was going to find it and adapt it to the selling process. Instead of selling one out of four copiers, I purposed to sell one out of one!

Needless to say, she thought I was a tad optimistic. The next day at the branch office my new boss asked me what my goals were and I told him that I intended to sell one out of one copier demonstrations. He thought I was nuts, but it was too late, he had already hired me! I searched the

Scriptures, especially the book of Proverbs, for eternal principles and enduring strategies that I could apply to the selling process, and then applied them to the best of my ability.

Ninety days later at my first quarterly sales review, I had to stand up in front of more than twenty of my peers and project my sales accomplishments on an overhead projector. I said, "I've been here for ninety days. In fact, this is my ninety-first day. I've done X amount of calls leading to twenty-two copier demonstrations, and I am pleased to tell you that I also have twenty-two sales." I had succeeded in selling one out of one copier demonstrations for a total of three-and-a-half times the number of copiers I was given as a goal—a goal that had never previously been achieved! Not only was this phenomenal for the company, but it was unprecedented in my sales career. The difference? I had found a way to successfully incorporate Biblical principles into the selling process. Suddenly, my results were dramatically better.

Sadly, many people question the validity of the selling profession and think that selling is a dirty word. They don't recognize it as neither moral nor immoral and refuse to grow in their understanding of it. Because of their lack of knowledge, they slowly grind away in their mediocrity, living well below their God-given potential. They slowly perish as their dreams continue to go unfulfilled.

What happened? Why would they settle for second best? The reason is that they were sold! Somewhere in life they bought into the lie that selling is something you do to people for your profit, rather than with them for mutual profit. Being decent people, they didn't want to play that game. They'd seen the wolves thriving in business arena virtually unchallenged and agonized internally over such prosperity, finally accepting the platitude that "nice guys finish last." After all, they would rather be a nice guy and finish last than be a wolf and finish first, as if finishing first and being a nice guy were somehow mutually exclusive.

In the grand game of commerce, wolves and sheep compete for the same slice of the economic pie. In preparation for the contest, wolves don sheep's apparel to ply their cunning ways under the cover of implied innocence while hiding the devious essence of their soul. Many sheep, on the other hand, have traded the innocence of their souls for the crafty ways of the wolf in a sorry attempt to level the playing field and win their "fair share" of business. At the end of the day, they've become sheep in wolves' clothing and recognize that the anguished, lonely howling they hear in the night is their own.

But wearing a wolf's clothing is not the only option. By walking close to the Shepherd, some have learned to compete boldly with the wolves. They know how to keep their sense of balance in a most uneven world without adapting the predatory habits of their fiercest competitors. They walk with confidence into the lairs of any corporate boardroom and do not flinch, because they know the Shepherd is with them and they've learned His ways. In sales, it's that kind of bold sheep that wins, and wolves move on to easier territory.

What this means is that nice guys can and should finish first! If you're a nice guy who's not finishing first, don't blame the wolf. Don't blame your company, product, economy, or customer. Look yourself square in the eye and accept full responsibility for your actions and results. There will always be "reasons" why something didn't work. Accepting them for your personal justification will be your downfall. Unless failure becomes an unacceptable option, it will become an unavoidable routine.

Selling is a worthy vocation. The wolves have marked out the territory with their reputation and for too long we have let them have their victories while we huddled under the banner of being "nice guys." It's my belief that wolves should never win, and when they do, the ground they take will remain contested until I take it back. And how will I take it back? Inevitably the wolf always reveals himself for who he really is—a self-serving, money grabbing predator. When that happens, his prey (the customer) will begin to look for a way out, and when they do, I'll be there anticipating their needs and offering solutions from a principle-based, value-added, customer-centered perspective.

The reason nice guys who succeed are accused of being wolves is because nice guys will go toe-to-toe with any wolf and not back down. The mild mannered sales reps who try to be nicer than Jesus are offended at this. Their pious attitude makes them easy prey for wolves. It isn't that nice guys are pushy, it's just that they're not pushovers! When they do push, it's always in the best interest of the customer. The wolf, on the other hand, pushes only for his own agenda: another day, another dollar.

Succeeding in sales is not about becoming a smarter wolf, a nicer wolf, a better wolf, or a Christian wolf. No, succeeding in sales is about outserving your competition in the best interest of your customers.

In short, succeeding in sales is about bringing to bear on the customers' behalf that which benefits them most in a bold, uncompromising manner. And when the wolves begin to howl in the night, the nice guys will sleep peacefully, knowing they've honored God, served their fellow man and been true to themselves.

Outserving is all about:

- discovering and meeting your customers' real needs,
- understanding their goals, dreams, and vision for the future,
- shouldering their burden and helping them get to their destination.
- not backing down from a ruthless competitor,
- hanging in there with customers, and
- walking them through their doubts, calming their fears, and solving their problems.

2

High Probability Selling

Have you ever wished you would only have to call on those people who were going to buy? Think of how much more effective you could be! But it doesn't work that way. There's something to learn about God and life in the struggle, and it will build character if we let it. However, we can greatly improve our effectiveness.

In the parable of the sower (Matthew 13), just under twenty percent of the seed yielded over eighty percent of the return. What did the nearly twenty percent of the seed have in common? They were all planted in good soil. Similarly, if you want to have outstanding success in sales, you must learn to identify good soil and plant your seed in that soil.

You can divide your prospects into four groups:

Group 1 — The "wayside" prospects are no more ready to buy your product than fly to the moon. You already know their profile, so don't invest your time there.

Group 2 — The "stony ground" prospects will act interested, but after you leave, they quickly lose heart. Their interest is shallow. You can recognize them on the first call because you were unable to find any real "pain." They express interest in your solution without having first admitted their pain (revelation of their need). They're nice people, but they won't come through with the commitment.

Group 3 — The "thorny ground" prospects look a bit more promising. They have evident needs, but are too caught up in substitute solutions that drain their cash, time and energy, thereby preventing you from reaping any significant result with them. They tend to look for the quick fix, the cheap price and the "too good to be true" kind of deal. They will admit pain during your initial interview, but you will find them hesitant to commit due to all their other pressing commitments. They are an emergency looking for a place to happen, but in the meantime, they've got a crisis to deal with, and it may or may not involve what you have to offer.

Group 4 — The "good ground" prospects are the ones who have genuine need, are willing to admit it, and are prepared to take action if and when a reasonable plan is offered to them. I haven't figured out exactly how to only call on this type of prospect, but you can choose to only present your product solution to them. Never waste your time presenting your solution to the first three kinds of prospect. Oh, it's true you might make a sale every once in a while, but while you're working in that field, the smarter sales reps are working the good ground and selling at a much higher rate. Only present your solution to a prospect where you and they see the need, and the solution you have makes sense and is obtainable for the prospect.

Another approach with your "good ground" group would be to target the twenty percent who make up eighty percent of your business. Experienced sales reps know it can take twice as long to make a thousand-dollar sale to a small sized customer than it does to make a twenty-thousand-dollar sale to a larger customer.

Create a profile of what a "good ground" prospect looks like, then create another profile of what the top twenty percent who bring you eighty percent of your business looks like. For example, if you're in the copier business, you're not going to spend much time calling on retail stores because you know they typically don't have the volume of need to justify the purchase, so concentrate on businesses with significant office staff, such as law offices, larger industrial companies, and realtors.

Then look at your customers who have brought you the most profitable business over the last few years. What do they look like? What do they have in common? How long was their buying cycle? What was it about your product or service that uniquely satisfied their need over what your competitor had to offer? Develop a strategy to target those prospects first. On the way to getting those sales, it's okay to spend time on some of the smaller opportunities, but make sure your time is spent where you will get the highest return for your effort.

On the way towards highest return, do not neglect entirely the smaller companies because God may have a plan for you to help the owner and because small companies often become big companies. We must always be sensitive to how God is directing on any given day. His priorities may be different than ours. I was once at a business to drop something off, hurrying on my way, when the owner's wife (who was in her seventies and looking near to death) asked me a question about my wife. Although I felt I didn't have time for a conversation, I stopped and talked with her. During that conversation, I let her know how much God loved her, and cared for her well-being. God used that conversation to touch her deeply. Later that day, my wife continued the conversation in even more detail. The owner's wife was encouraged and uplifted, and we received a similar blessing by showing her respect.

The strategies and principles that can help you excel in sales are simple, but they do not comprise a complete package. Prayer is also an important ingredient. Several years ago I was with my boss in a government office trying to close a sale. The equipment we had placed on trial had performed so poorly that we had to replace it twice during the trial period. The competition was begging for an opportunity to compete with us and we wanted to shut them out and close the sale. We knew our offer was the best choice for them, but it was easy to understand how they might have felt a little insecure about it.

After my boss and I had been with the city manager and his secretary for about an hour, it was apparent that we were at an impasse. I politely stepped out of the office and went into the room where the trial copier had been installed and began to pray—fervently! I asked God to help these people see that we were working in their best interest and that we would take the best care of them. I asked Him to calm their fears about doing business with us. While I was still praying, my boss came running into the room where I was standing and said, "What are you doing?" I told him I was praying. He looked at me in the most unusual way, then said, "Well, get back in here. They've suddenly changed their minds and they want to proceed and I don't know the specific numbers." God cleared away their fears and they saw our proposition in a much more positive light—and we walked out of there with the order.

I was such a firm believer in the effectiveness of prayer that once I identified "good ground" prospects, I would carry their names on individual 3x5 cards and pray for them almost everyday on my way to work. I didn't believe they would suddenly wake up one day and call me to order my product, but I did believe God could give me favor with them and wisdom from above so that I might better discern their real needs and present my case in a compelling manner. I recommend the same to you.

3

Four Cornerstones of Sales Success

Succeeding in sales is a multi-dimensional challenge. You must know, understand, and be competent in four distinct disciplines if you hope to achieve long lasting success in the field of sales. Each discipline works in harmony with and accentuates your growing application of the other dimensions.

Dimension 1— Strategy

The first dimension is the discipline of strategy. Strategy is based upon knowledge. Your ability to succeed will be greatly hampered or helped by your knowledge of the following five topics:

1. Your product or service:

Become an expert on what you have to offer! Most companies are strong on this point with sales training consisting almost entirely of communicating the virtues of the product or service being provided. But even with this, I often see a profound weakness among sales reps who don't understand their product well. If you want to improve your selling strength, make a list of the main products or services you do offer, and then prepare an in-depth presentation of each item you listed. If necessary, get technical support from in-house sources, then present what you have learned at the next sales meeting, to your sales manager, or even at home to your spouse.

You'll find in preparing to teach a subject you will learn far more than you would have by simply preparing to learn about it. This is important because the more you know about what you have to offer, the more secure you can make your prospects feel and the more respect you will gain in their eyes. We all want to deal with people who really know their stuff, so give yourself a leg up and become an expert in your field. Do you really understand what makes your product unique to the marketplace? What makes it stand out? Can you articulate that in a clear and compelling manner? Spend some time getting better acquainted with your product or service.

2. Your competition:

The early church fathers serve as a great model because they preached the gospel against tremendous spiritual opposition and made substantial gains against their adversary, the devil. Throughout their letters to the early church it is evident that they were not "ignorant of the devil's devices" (II Corinthians 2:11) and wrestled or competed with him for the souls of men. Likewise in business, when you are informed, instead of ignorant of the devices or plans of your competition, you will know not only what you're up against but how they ply their trade. That knowledge will allow you to offer the offsetting advantages of your product or service in a manner that can neutralize or at least minimize the impact of your competitor on your prospect.

One of my prospects had a competitor's copier on trial and was suitably impressed with it. Naturally, he wanted me to match their offer before he would consider testing our equipment. The prospect told me that my competitor had offered him a free sixty-day trial period to evaluate the copier. My company never offered more than a three or four-day trial and usually a day or two was sufficient. I recognized that my boss would never go for it, but I also knew my competition and felt certain that the prospect misunderstood the offer that had been made to him. Our competition did indeed have a sixty-day trial, but you had to first sign a two-year agreement and then you were later billed for the sixty-day trial period. Not only did I know that to be a fact, but also I had in my briefcase a copy of our competition's standard agreement. I pulled it out and helped my customer see that he had misunderstood the agreement. He then pulled out his own contract, which was identical to the one I had, and conceded the point. On the spot he ordered our standard trial evaluation and by the end of the week we had a sale. Without knowing the competition, a less informed sales rep might have capitulated and offered a free sixty-day trial or simply lost the opportunity altogether, blaming it on the aggressive actions of a stronger competitor.

You should know who your major competitors are and what product or service they are offering. You should know their value proposition (the unique value offering they are propositioning the market with) and how they are positioning themselves in your market. If possible, you should know their pricing, along with the strengths and weaknesses of their product or service. By gaining this information, you establish yourself as an expert in your field and your prospect will pay more attention and give more credence to what you have to say.

3. Your industry:

Become an industry expert. If you don't have the interest to do that, you're probably in the wrong business. Find out what trends are developing. Do you attend trade shows? Do you read industry publications? Have you ever tried writing for them? Consider writing an article for a trade magazine. It will enhance your credibility with potential clients. Is your industry going through major change, such as deregulation? How will this affect your customers? How well are you poised to deal with the change?

4. Your trade:

Have you mastered the sales trade? Do you purchase books or tapes to further your sales education? Do you have a well-planned questioning strategy? Do you know why people buy? Do you understand the buying process? Do you know how to deliberately create a climate of trust? Have you refined your proposal development and writing skills? Do you have purpose to every call or do you just call on customers because it's the second Tuesday of the month and you always call them the second Tuesday of every month? What about your presentation skills? Have you studied and practiced the art of logic and rhetoric? What about closing skills? Are you skilled at helping people come to a successful conclusion about your product or service?

5. Your customers and prospects:

How much do you know about your customers? Once I was doing a customized sales training program for a company with about 85 sales people when I asked one of the experienced sales veterans, "Tell me about one of your manufacturing customers that you've sold to recently."

He was able to tell me what city and state they were in and what they purchased and for how much, but when I asked him what his customer manufactured, he couldn't tell me.

He'd been going in their facility for years but had never even paid attention to what it was that they did. Without knowing what they produced, there was no way he could keep up with the changes their industry was going through.

He couldn't hope to add extra value by being an additional source of helpful and reliable knowledge. He couldn't even realistically hope that the customer would see him as a concerned vendor because he had never taken enough interest to ask about their business, let alone show enough interest to look around.

Customer loyalty to a vendor goes no deeper than the sales rep's loyalty to them. When the competition calls and takes a sincere interest in what's important to the customer, the indifference of the existing vendor will surface and that customer will have found a new vendor. Sadly, the sales rep will probably not even notice the loss until the competitor is firmly lodged in that customer's business.

When you have a depth of knowledge in these areas, you can formulate an effective strategy for gaining market share. When you combine what you know about your product, industry, competition, customers and trade, your strategy begins to take shape. That strategy should include a good understanding of how to uniquely position yourself and your company, product, or service in the customer's mind to create a clear, lasting and compelling reason to choose you over your competitors.

Develop a strategy to consistently uncover your prospects' highest needs. Have a well thought out line of questioning that reliably uncovers need, exposes pain and sets the stage for your product or service. Your strategy should include preparing a list of the top ten objections you regularly encounter and the most well thought answers you can provide, including third-party stories, written testimonials and other forms of evidence you can prepare to answer any objections. Based on what you know about your competition, you should have a line of questioning that will unveil their weakest points. Be careful here. Never tell customers something you can ask them. In other words, never tell them about the weaknesses of their current suppliers. Instead, ask them focused questions that when answered will reveal in their own words their suppliers' relative weaknesses. Have a logical flow to your questioning and your presentation to lead your customers along the continuum at their pace to a strategically pre-planned conclusion.

Dimension 2 – Skill

The second dimension is the discipline of skill. In sales, skill is the ability to harness raw motivational energy, knowledge and strategy in order to generate sales. Without skill, activity accomplishes little, motivation grows weary, strategies fall by the wayside and principles have little effect. To succeed in sales, you must become skilled in the basic elements of your trade. Those elements include: planning skills, the ability to spark interest, develop rapport, establish respect and create trust, questioning skills, listening skills, negotiating skills, problem solving skills, closing skills, and more. All these elements need to be studied and practiced, much like a professional golfer who practices everything from long distance drives to putting. What are you doing to improve your skill? You need to deliberately and purposefully apply what you learn until it's a part of what you do and how you function. Better yet, find a friend or co-worker with a similar interest in sales and work on developing your skills together.

I know of a man who practiced and developed his skill, then walked into an office on the chance that a manager might have time to see him. He met with the decision-maker, and by utilizing his knowledge and skill, he walked out with what would net his company $350,000 to $1,000,000 in the next twelve months.

Dimension 3 — Motivation

The third dimension of successful selling is motivation and attitude. Motivation is the raw energy driving every successful sales professional. Without motivation, nothing moves, skills deteriorate, strategies gather dust and principles have nothing to empower. It has everything to do with what you believe about things. What do you believe about your company? Do you believe they can compete effectively in the marketplace? Do you believe in their approach to the market? Do you really believe your product or service is the best choice for your customers? Do you believe in the claims made by your company about the product or service you sell? What about the competition? Do you believe they are better priced, of better quality or in some way superior to your offering? Are you intimidated by them? Do you believe they use dishonest or unethical means to secure business? What about your customers or prospects? Some salesmen feel that "all buyers are liars." What do you believe about your customers? Do you believe they don't have the budget, means, or need to buy your product? What about yourself? What do you believe about you, your chances of success or your strengths and weaknesses? Have you overestimated your weaknesses and underestimated your strengths, or vice versa? What do you believe about your potential, about the opportunities and challenges that lay ahead? What do you believe about your profession or industry? If you feel you "peddle" insurance as one man told me, then you need to find a line of work you can believe in.

What is attitude? Attitude is a deep-seated, chosen belief, either positive or negative, that sets in motion corresponding behavior, generally resulting in a self-fulfilling prophecy. If you have a negative attitude or belief about your competition that says, for example, "They always win because they deceive the customer and lie about their offer," then you'll likely react in a self-defeating way that sets them up for victory. If you don't like the results you're getting in the marketplace, take a close look at what you believe about your circumstances. Challenge those beliefs. Challenge their right to control your destiny and limit your success. It may be true that your competitor lies and deceives customers, but that doesn't mean you have to bow out. The truth is always more powerful than a lie. You can learn how to exploit their propensity for lying. The very thing that causes you loss in the marketplace can become the point of victory if you learn how to take advantage of it. You understand the fundamental flaw of being unethical in the marketplace: it doesn't work in the long run. Your job is to lead your customers to this understanding through a logical questioning process that allows them to draw the conclusions that are extremely obvious to you. This takes skill, fueled by motivation, guided by principle and navigated with strategy.

Dimension 4 – Principles

The fourth dimension of successful selling is having a principle-based approach. Principles give purpose and direction to your energy and abilities, empowering you to achieve levels of excellence and fulfillment otherwise unobtainable. Without principles, results achieved by skill and motivation alone have little meaning at the end of the day. Principles of trust, respect, love, justice, mercy, humility, honesty, and integrity are the guiding lights to govern our actions in the marketplace. To the extent that we embrace and uphold these principles, we move toward either stability or instability.

Selling skills are like golf skills in the sense that you can be taught them, but it may take a lifetime to be fully changed by them. Principles, on the other hand, are received by the mind like a napkin absorbs water. The water immediately affects all other aspects of the napkin, changing its appearance, its feel and its weight upon impact. When you grab hold of the significance of principles and begin to consciously incorporate them in a practical and deliberate way, you can see immediate impact on your sales results.

Several years ago a man in Florida called to say that he had just been let go from his salaried job and the only job he could find was in commission sales, selling satellite dishes in residential neighborhoods. He was scared to death because he had never sold before and he was going to be starting his job on Monday. He said, "Tell me what I need to know." We spoke for over an hour as I condensed and explained several principles in selling. He hung up, promising to call me back at the end of his first week.

When he called back, he was ecstatic. He had made eight presentations his first week and was able to incorporate the principles we had discussed over the phone with remarkable results. He closed eight sales and earned over three thousand dollars! When skills and principles are adapted practically in an honorable way, the results are tremendous.

4

The Motivation Secrets
of the
Ten Commandments

Remember the judge in the South who refused an order to take down a display of the Ten Commandments in his courtroom? His case attracted a lot of attention and provoked many people to speak up for their right to post the Ten Commandments, but my question is this: "Can you list in order the Ten Commandments?" I have found that hardly one in a hundred can do it!

The Ten Commandments are the central values of our faith and yet less than one percent can remember them, much less expound on their ramification to commerce, politics, or life. After much study, I have come to find that the Ten Commandments actually guard and protect ten legitimate motivational needs we all have. Being able to recognize these needs in others makes you better equipped to serve those needs within the context of your product or service offering. Cooperating with and selling to the hidden motivational needs protected by each commandment actually increases the level of cooperation you receive from your customers. On the other hand, ignoring these legitimate motivational needs can hinder your opportunities for success with clients without you ever knowing why.

I
You shall have no other gods before Me.

This commandment guards and protects our legitimate need for significance. Genesis 1:26 records that God said, "Let us make man in our image." When God made you and me in His image, He gave us our image and thus our identity. Our significance comes in large part from where we get our identity. If our identity comes from apes, as Darwin would have had us believe, then our sense of significance is greatly diminished.

How significant is it to think you evolved slowly from a slime pit to a lizard, to a bird and ultimately to an ape? That's not exactly a noble beginning. But what if you found that you had descended from royalty? That would be much more encouraging. We were made in God's image

(He is the King of Kings) and He has a good future in store for us (Jeremiah 29:11). Now that's significant!

We will worship whatever gives us our sense of identity and makes us feel truly significant. America's number one addiction is not drugs, alcohol or sex, it's the addiction to significance. People are desperate to feel significant. If money makes them feel significant, they will worship money by submitting to its demands and sacrificing friends, family and principle to acquire it. If being seen with famous people makes them feel significant, they will go out of their way to worship them, buying the merchandise they sell, lining up for an autograph or photo, and keeping themselves "in the know" about their favorite stars. So many people have lost sight of the fact that we get our identity and our image from God, and therefore get our significance from Him. They wander through life searching for ways to feel significant.

The more we know God, and not just about Him, the more we discover our true identity. And as we begin to comprehend the love He has for us, our sense of significance is greatly enhanced.

How does this apply to sales? A sale is about meeting needs, one of which is the need to feel significant. The question is how can God—through you—make this person feel significant? A good example of this is the Green Hills Grille in Nashville, Tennessee, one of my favorite restaurants. The atmosphere is relaxed, yet cultured. The food is exquisite, yet down home, and the service is impeccable. One way they demonstrate their high level of service is by greeting you by your name when you walk in the door. It makes me feel like an unexpected but highly welcome guest. It's the only restaurant that I frequent where the hosts have made the effort to remember the names of the patrons, which makes you feel kind of significant, and that's a nice feeling. In your business, look for simple ways you can make the people you deal with feel significant. It can return big dividends.

Concerning significance, it is also important to reflect on your conduct to see if you do or say anything that might make the other person feel insignificant. Being slow to return a call, late for an appointment, too casual with your approach, or simply not paying attention to what is being said can make someone feel slighted or insignificant. If you don't like where you stand with your customers or prospects, carefully consider where you may have made them feel insignificant. Then look for ways you can demonstrate their significance by treating them the way you would want to be treated if the shoe were on the other foot. Don't underestimate the need for significance.

II
You shall not make for yourself any graven image to worship or serve.

This commandment guards and protects our legitimate need for authority. We were created to be in authority over some things while always being under the authority of God. This is an important boundary, but if men are left to define God's boundaries by making graven images, they are submitting to and giving authority to something other than God.

The key to having authority is being under authority. When we choose not to be under authority, we lose our legitimate authority. Understanding the principles of authority allows us to work within God's order of establishing, honoring, and respecting other people's authority. When we do this correctly, we gain favor in the marketplace. This is an important lesson to learn, especially if you're trying to gain the favor of others. We have been wired since Creation to have authority. Prospective customers are wired for authority too, but if you don't recognize their legitimate authority boundaries, you can torpedo your chances of winning their favor. For example, if you go over their head in business without honoring their legitimate position and authority, they may make it difficult for you to proceed in that company.

Make it a point to recognize the legitimate sphere of authority your contacts have. Honor that authority and it will enhance their sense of significance and open doors for you. Violate that authority and it will diminish their sense of significance and they may in turn show you how important they really are by sabotaging your sale.

III

You shall not take the name of the Lord your God in vain.

This commandment goes far beyond refraining from profanity. It protects our legitimate need for honor. God's name is to be honored through our words and actions. When we apply God's name to our agenda, we dishonor God. Many people have applied God's name to their vision and when the vision falls apart, it brings dishonor to the name of God and to them.

But God intended us for honor. He promised in Proverbs that humility and the fear of the Lord bring riches, honor and life. He wired us with a legitimate need for honor. When you understand this in the business arena, you can begin to ask, "How can I honor my customers in a way that glorifies God and enhances their significance?" When people feel they're significant to you, they're much more likely to give you their willing cooperation.

You can begin by avoiding the practice of dishonoring them or applying their name to your agenda. For example, when you keep telling your customers how much they need what you have and how much better off they will be with your product or service, and all the while you can only think of the commission you will earn from this sale, there's a good chance you're dishonoring them. You're really thinking of yourself first but pretending to be putting them first. That's dishonoring, and they can usually detect it and will offer resistance. Honor your customers, listen to their needs, and discover their pain. Put yourself in their shoes, and if you still feel that what you have to offer is in their best interest, you honor them by serving them your product. The income you earn is merely a healthy by-product of a job well-done.

Everyone has an inner need to feel honored. When we're honored, we feel significant, and when we feel significant, we are much more likely to cooperate with those doing the honoring. In business, there are many practical ways you can honor someone. I had a barber once named Dave who every time I showed up for a haircut would make a big deal out of my arrival and communicate to all the customers and co-workers how honored he was to have my business. He made me feel like a celebrity.

But people would ask me, "Who cuts your hair?" and before I could answer, they would usually offer the name of the person they were using. In other words, they didn't feel I had a very good haircut, but I never changed barbers. Why? Because Dave made me feel honored. And when people feel honored, it enhances their significance. When you help someone feel significant, they're much more likely to do business with you, even if there are better options elsewhere.

IV

Remember the Sabbath Day to keep it holy.

Man was not made for the Sabbath, Jesus said, but the Sabbath was made for man (Mark 2:27). The Sabbath is set aside as a way of recognizing man's need for rest. Rest is not just a physical need; it is very much an emotional need. The fourth commandment actually guards and protects our legitimate need for rest and peace of mind.

We're called to extend God's Kingdom in the marketplace, which is all about having a right standing with God, resulting in peace and joy in the Holy Spirit. Does your line of work add to or take away from your customers' peace of mind? Does your product or service put them in financial bondage, or does it contribute to their peace of mind? If your line of work is at cross-purposes with God's purposes, you might want to consider something different. Maybe He'd even bless it!

This is important to understand, especially if you'd like to grow your business by meeting the real needs of people. For example, suppose you sell expensive office equipment. It's natural that people are going to offer resistance to your price, because the greater the investment, the greater the risk, and the more risk, the less peace of mind people have. So now that you know that peace of mind is something that God sanctions, how can you in your business proposal reduce their risk and/or increase their peace of mind?

You can reduce risk by including "risk reversals" such as extended warranties, replacement guarantees, or a generous refund policy. You can increase peace of mind by helping your customers fully understand the long-term benefits of your equipment, which may include time savings, enhanced image, more business for them, etc. Lastly, you can put the price difference in perspective. When you spread the price difference over the life of their investment, it probably reduces to a few dollars a week, maybe even pennies a day. By putting the price in perspective, you lower their risk threshold and increase their peace of mind.

V

Honor your father and mother.

Growing up under our parents' authority guards and protects our legitimate motivational need for security. Legitimate authority creates a sense of security for those submitted to it. We were born with an innate need to feel secure and that need didn't end when we got out on our own. If you put children in a playground with no fence, they won't know where the boundaries are and on average will tend to stay in the middle of the playground. Give them some boundaries, like a fence, and they'll play all over the playground and even hang on the edge of the fence. Giving them boundaries gives them security. You need it, I need it, and your customers need it.

If you have customers who seem a little insecure about your business proposition, then consider the possibility that they haven't seen the boundaries and therefore can't fairly evaluate the risk. Perhaps they're wondering what risks they will be exposed to and/or protected from if they take a step. It's in your best interest to define the risks up front. In so doing, you remove any ambiguity, you show them where the fence line is, and you show them how far you are willing to go to protect them. The more security you're able to provide and define, the more likely you are to have a successful outcome. Anticipate their need for security and prepare to answer their concerns in advance. You might say something like, "I know this seems like quite an investment and indeed it is. That's why we've included this ironclad guarantee that ensures your continued protection regardless of market conditions. And that's what you really want, isn't it?" In a simple statement you've addressed a certain insecurity while simultaneously adding to their security.

When you make people feel secure by recognizing their natural insecurities, you show respect and ultimately enhance their sense of significance, which is protected by the first commandment. And when you do that you're much more likely to have a successful outcome.

VI
You shall not murder.

Cain killed his brother, Abel. He hated and rejected him, which is always at the core of murder. The opposite of hate and rejection is love and acceptance, which are the legitimate motivational needs we all have that are protected by this Commandment. When we go into the marketplace to compete with our products, services and ideas, it helps to understand what motivates people. People naturally want to feel loved and accepted, but how do you appropriately make a potential customer feel loved? First, what is love and how can you demonstrate it practically? Jesus said, "Greater love has no one than this, than to lay down one's life for his friends" (John 15:13).

Love is demonstrated when we yield our rights for the benefit of others. We temporarily lay a little of our life down to enhance someone else's life experience. It is called service. I don't mean the obligatory, reluctant type of service you might expect from an unhappy bureaucrat in a government job. I'm talking about outrageous service. The kind of service that makes the customers say, "WOW!" It's the kind of service that anticipates needs and makes preparation. Kind of like the Lamb of God who came not to be served, but to serve, and to die for us. Now that's love!

Acceptance is also an integral part of this Commandment. All too often in sales we feel it's our job to persuade people of our point of view before we understand their position. We think that if we accept their point of view, we somehow diminish our chances of success. Make your potential customer feel accepted, remove the sense of threat that comes from intolerance of their opinion, and let them know there's room for a different opinion. You will be in for some very positive feedback! I believe that my audio coaching program is second to none, but some might not agree. That's all right. If they give the program a chance and don't like it, they can return it for a full refund. Guess what? By accepting people with their different opinions and eliminating the risk with my money back guarantee, I create a healthy climate for doing business. The result is one of the lowest return-rates in the industry.

Make those with differing opinions welcome. It leads to dialogue, and dialogue leads to understanding, and understanding leads to cooperation, which is the foundation for successfully conducting business.

VII
You shall not commit adultery.

The 7th Commandment is obvious in its meaning, but its implications are far reaching. This commandment actually guards and protects our legitimate motivational need for preference. When we marry someone, we're to forsake all other romantic loves and prefer our spouse above all other human relationships. We're called to leave our parents and cleave to our spouse (Genesis 2:24). In short, we're to give our spouse preference. God made us to want to be preferred and intends for that need to be met in the fullest way in the sacred bonds of matrimony.

I prefer my wife over my job and over all other relationships. She actually expects it, but that's okay with me, because I expect it, want it, and receive it from her in return. Knowing that we all have a motivational need for preference enables us to ask,

"How can God through me in this business transaction help make this person feel preferred in a legitimate way that doesn't usurp the spousal relationship?" Remember, when you make people feel preferred, they feel significant, and when they feel significant in your eyes, they're much more likely to do business with you.

The need for preference is common to us all. Who doesn't want to be loved by someone in a way that supersedes all others? And to a lesser extent, who wouldn't enjoy a complimentary upgrade to first class seating on an overseas flight? The question is, "How we can apply what we know about our basic motivational needs to the business process?" Is there a legitimate way to make customers feel preferred? Look at American Express. They have a basic credit card you can use for an annual fee of around $50, a gold one for around $100, and a platinum card for a few hundred dollars. Sure, they give you a few extra perks, but they are providing basically the same service while allowing those who wish to pay more, the privilege of feeling preferred. Airlines show preference to their frequent fliers with free first class upgrades. Grocery stores give pricing advantages to those who carry their special cards. Some restaurants and coffee shops give out free sandwiches and coffee to their frequent customers. It's all about preference, which is a powerful way to develop customer loyalty and a powerful way to win in the marketplace.

VIII
You shall not steal.

This commandment applies to more than your local burglar. It actually guards and protects our legitimate need to acquire. Mankind has a built-in need to acquire things. If owning things was a sin, that would make God the biggest sinner of all, being that He owns it all. He made us in His image and gave us His likeness. Yes, we all fell through Adam's sin, but He has made us a new creature and has given us the mind of Christ.

Theft cuts to the core of our legitimate need to acquire. It steals away from us that which is protected by God's law. People in sales steal anytime they extract more from customers than is agreed to. Anytime they pad the order with a few extra expenses, without the customers' knowledge, they steal. When customers sense their "need to acquire" is being threatened, you lose the right to have their business, not to mention the right to look yourself in the mirror and feel good about what you see.

Knowing that God wired man with a need and a will to acquire, how can you through your business dealings legitimately tap into this need to help more people obtain the product or service you offer, while simultaneously helping them have their needs met? My father had a long and illustrious career in sales. The work he loved was fueled by integrity and crowned with success. Around the time of his 80th birthday, I asked him what understanding helped him more than anything else to succeed in sales. Honesty and integrity were a given, so he simply told me that if he could ever show customers how he could either save them money or make them money with his product, he would usually make the sale. When he sold fire extinguishers during the Great Depression, he showed them how it would lower their insurance premiums. When he sold bowling alley equipment in the sixties, he showed them how they could make money with their investment.

In your line of work, ask yourself how what you have to offer can generate a positive economic impact. If your product is more expensive, there's probably a good reason for it and that reason may have economic consequences over time, such as longer life, fewer breakdowns, or greater convenience. Help your customers see the favorable economic consequences and you will significantly increase your chances of success.

IX
You shall not bear false witness against your neighbor.

This guards and protects a person's legitimate motivational need to be understood and to understand correctly. This begins with telling the truth and though it seems simple enough, it's very easy to make truthful statements while deliberately conveying a lie.

In sales it's critically important to not only tell the truth, but to tell the whole truth. Practice full disclosure. It is so easy to mislead someone by withholding pertinent information. A customer asks if he can get out of the lease agreement and the salesman says, "Yes." What isn't mentioned is the fact that the leasing company will assess a penalty equaling the full value of the contract. In sales, remember that people have a legitimate need to be understood and to understand. Help your customers understand the full picture and lead them through a well-informed, decision making process. They'll thank you for it with their business more often than not.

I've also learned in business that customers expect you to understand them. In fact, most people seem to expect you to view their circumstances through their personal grid and can get upset when you don't see things their way. With this knowledge, how can you help meet your customers' legitimate need to be understood? You can start by asking lots of questions and then really listening to the answers. While talking with your customers, ask them about their goals and how they view life.

Learning to really understand your customers will help you express your offer in language and with illustrations that will assure your customers that you truly understand and can help them.

X
You shall not covet.

The 10th Commandment guards and protects our legitimate motivational need to enjoy contentment. Contentment is being satisfied with what you do have, while covetousness is thinking you'll be satisfied with what you don't have.

In sales, part of your job is helping your customers gain contentment with what is within their reach. To do this you'll need to discover areas of discontent that your customers currently have. They may be experiencing poor service or inferior quality with their current product or service provider. Lead them through the process of discovery to expose their discontentment. Once you understand this, you have a basis to build your case for your product or service.

Show them how your product or service meets or exceeds their stated need. You might say, "You mentioned that you were experiencing a two week turnaround on your test results and were losing customers as a result, costing you an estimated $50,000 per year. I can understand how distressing that loss must be. With our guaranteed 72-hour turnaround, you'll not only never have to worry about that loss again, but you can look forward to gaining new business from your competitor's customer base. That's what you really want, isn't it?"

Lead your customers down the path of contentment. Paint the picture in clear unambiguous terms and you will enjoy greater success.

5

Research, Evaluate, Strategize & Test

When the Israelites were considering invading the land of Canaan , they sent out a reconnaissance team of twelve men to spy out the land. They were given a specific set of questions that they were to bring home answers for. The leadership team of Israel, headed up by Moses, wanted that information to plan out a strategy. When the spies got back, they shared their report with the people. The facts were evaluated, the original strategy was set aside, and the people spent the next forty years being tested in the desert wilderness because of their wrong decision.

Forty years later, they dusted off their strategy and began to execute it. Their plan was not complex, yet it was so effective that it has been taught in military schools ever since. It's called, "divide and conquer." The Israelites attacked the central highlands, cutting off effective communication between the northern and southern regions of Canaan. They then divided themselves by tribe, cleaned up local resistance and took possession of the land.

Preparation

Preparation is key before engaging in a battle for the marketplace, but if you prepare well, you will find rest for your soul. Here is an acronym to help you remember the four steps of preparation:

R   Research
E   Evaluate
S   Strategize
T   Test

Before the Israelites devised a plan, they had to identify the opportunity. They were approximately three million strong, coming out of slavery in Egypt and in need of a homeland. They had identified the land, which God had promised to Abraham as flowing with milk and honey where every man would eat from his own vine, sit under his own fig tree and drink waters from his own cistern. They didn't set their eyes on Europe or Africa. All they wanted was what God had promised their father

Abraham. In sales, it's also very important to identify your target market and focus your efforts towards that market. Build a plan around securing that market and follow it well.

Planning Rule 1:
Begin with the end in mind

When devising a territory strategy, you should begin with the end in mind. The Lamb of God "was slain from the foundation of the world" (Revelation 13:8), which clearly shows that it was not an emergency last minute rescue. The atonement on the Cross was planned from the very beginning! What is your long-term plan for your territory and your individual customers? Are you selling to sell again? Are you developing customer loyalty? Are you building a strong referral base? Are you leveraging from your past sales successes to secure new ones by obtaining written testimonials or securing their permission to be a referral for you? Your plan should go beyond making the sale to your customer and include converting that customer into a spokesman for you, your product and your company.

What is the end result you have in mind when you walk in your customer's front door or call on the phone? Over the years, I've gone on sales calls to evaluate a sales team for a client. I usually ask the sales rep why we're calling on a certain customer and the answers are usually something like, "It's Tuesday. I always drop by to see him the second Tuesday of each month." Too many sales reps think they are doing their customers a favor by "dropping by," but I've got news for them: their customers are busy when they show up and don't need another interruption in their day unless it is of benefit to them.

When I owned a small publishing company, I used to have a salesman call on me "whenever he was in town." At first I was glad to see him, because he had some sample stock that was of interest to me. After awhile, however, it became obvious that I was just another name he could put on his call report to justify his trip to my town. I stopped the visits and told him I'd call him if I needed his services. If, on the other hand, he had showed up with something of interest and relevance to my business, I would have welcomed his visits.

When you feel the need to call on customers with some level of frequency, make a point of finding something you can bring them or tell them that will help them with their goals. Bring a newspaper article related to their industry or turn them on to another vendor (non-competitive to you) that will help them with their business. You can combine your sales call with a personal delivery of something they have recently ordered. Get creative, be thoughtful, and put yourself in their shoes. Give them a reason to look forward to the second Tuesday of each month!

Another reason for seeing a customer I often hear is, "I sent him a quote and I want to see if he's made a decision yet." Think about it. If the customer had made a decision in your favor, he would very likely have called you already. If he made a decision in your competitor's favor, you're probably too late. If he's still undecided, just showing up and asking if he's made a decision will likely yield you a simple, "No." Instead, consider calling in advance and telling the customer that you have some important additional information you would like to review briefly with him. It might be something as simple as an alternative payment plan, a variation on a trade-in policy or a possible enhancement of your delivery schedule. Then, when you're in front of the customer, if he's already decided in your favor, you still win. If he's decided in favor of the competition, you have come prepared with additional ammunition to cause them to reconsider. If he's undecided when you show up, you have come prepared with something that could put them over the top. No matter how you slice it, you bring more to the table and increase your chances of success.

Planning Rule 2:
Less is more

Some argue that less is not more. This is based on the belief that selling is merely a numbers game. Though there is a definite relationship between the amount of activity you initiate and the amount of results you generate, there's much more to it. For example, Jesus was constantly thinning out the crowds with statements like, "eat my flesh" and "drink my blood" (John 6:54). He didn't seem to be interested in attracting large crowds or recruiting huge numbers of disciples. He selected twelve men, of which he poured more into just three.

When I sold twenty-two copiers out of twenty-two demonstrations in my first ninety days, the company was not 100% satisfied. Yes, I had sold far more than was even imagined, but I had failed to do the twenty-five to forty demonstrations they thought I should have done in that same time period. In fact, to close twenty-two sales, according to them, I should have done eighty-eight demonstrations. Funny how folly always has to justify its offspring. Wisdom, on the other hand, produces fruit that always justifies the branch. My idea was simple: I would pour more of my time and resources into a fewer number of qualified prospects. The results spoke for themselves. I would treat each customer like they were the most important thing on my agenda. I gave them a lot of personal attention. I planned, researched, evaluated and strategized for each customer. Sure, it took more of my time per customer, but I wasn't after demonstrations, I was after sales. Don't chase activity, chase results. Activity is not the goal—results are the goal. Plan your activities according to your goals.

Planning Rule 3:
Quality begets quantity

Quality seeds produce a quality harvest. A high quality, white diamond will bring far more than a dozen yellow diamonds. Quality work and quality effort will always yield more than mere quantity will. This does not mean less effort, but rather, better effort. Better in the sense that more thought and planning have gone into it. Better in the sense that the customers can discern that they are receiving a higher quality of service. When you make a better effort instead of merely more effort, you will see a greater return on your investment of time. If you pursue more effort, you may get a little more result, but you may have less if you provided a lower level of service to get the higher number of calls. More activity may look good on a sales report, but at the end of the day, only results matter to the company. Give them what they want (results) by giving the customers what they want: quality attention to their needs.

Now that you have decided to begin with the end in mind and deliver better service to your prospects and customers, it's time to look a little closer at the four steps of preparation.

STEP ONE: Research

When you want to win over a significant account to your company, it is important to learn as much about your customers as possible. Start with company records on file. What kind of account history do you have on record? Have they ever done business with your company before? What's their buying history? Payment record? Who in your company has had dealings with them before? Talk to former customers and find out why they're no longer a customer. Research the Internet. Find out about their business, industry and product. Talk with other vendors who may already have a favorable relationship with them. Who do you know who might already have them as a customer who would make a favorable introduction for you? Who in your circle of acquaintances can give you an inside view of their turf?

STEP TWO: Evaluate

Once you have gathered the relevant information, it's time to evaluate it. What important information is missing? What would you like to know before contacting them that you don't know now? Who can give you that information? Where can you find that person? What does the absence of that information imply? What would having it tell you? Based on this information, what needs may the customers have that you should anticipate? Based on what you've discovered, what objections might you encounter? With whom can you speak to help interpret what you've uncovered?

STEP THREE: Strategize

Now that you've gathered information and evaluated the implications of what you've found, it's time to develop a strategy. What resources will you utilize to help you gain entry into the account? What will you use to create enough interest for the prospects to agree to an appointment with you? What will you say in your first meeting to create sufficient interest to proceed with the rest of the call? What questions will you ask to lead you to the information you need to help them? What kind of evidence will you need to support you in your call? What exactly do you hope to accomplish in your first contact? What is the minimum goal you have for that call? What's the best-case scenario? Think through a well-planned response to likely objections you may hear.

STEP FOUR: Test

This is simple. Role-play the call with a co-worker, friend, or family member. At the very least, rehearse it with yourself. Create a path you want to follow and rehearse it until you are familiar with it. Know your questions, answers, evidence, and objectives well. Be prepared to relate relevant third party stories. Become comfortable with word pictures and analogies that will help you communicate clearly the most important points you will be making. In short, be a professional. Treat selling like a professional career and you will be rewarded with a professional's income!

6

Understanding Need—
Before You Proceed

As you already know, seed falls on many different types of soil, but only good soil will produce a good return on a farmer's investment. You have to know the soil before you plant. In sales, this means you have to know the need before you can proceed. I've always wished I could call on companies that needed my service when I called on them, but that's not how things work. There is a natural process of refinement that I must bring my prospects through before I can meet their needs.

I begin by focusing my efforts on likely prospects, but even then, not all recognize or believe they have a need, but without a need, I won't proceed. What I consider a need and what someone else considers a need may be two different things. For example, some people need a reliable form of transportation and others think they need a brand new Mercedes. I decided a long time ago not to make value judgments on what other people consider needs. If they want a deluxe model when the budget model will do fine, it is your duty as the car salesman to inform them of those facts, but let them decide what they want.

Levels of Buying Need

No pain, no need, no plan

This is where a buyer currently has needs taken care of and truly cannot benefit from your product or service at this time. The sooner you can recognize this and bow out, the better for both of you.

Suppressed pain, no hope of plan

One scenario of this is where the buyer has been living with the pain so long that he is used to it and doesn't see it as a problem. I made a call with one of my client's sales reps who sold management consulting services to industrial companies. The salesman I was with had failed to help the prospect get in touch with his pain. We were about to bow out when I asked the prospect about his back. I had noticed that he was unable to stand straight and he explained that he had lived with that problem for about 18 years and didn't even notice it anymore. He was convinced there was nothing anyone could do for him. I told him that it was easy for me to detect his back pain because of my history with back problems and how this whole discussion was similar to his business in that it was reasonably apparent there were some pain issues with his company that he had gotten used to. He didn't believe there was a good solution and had adapted himself to the current conditions. I assured him we couldn't help his back pain, but we could bring him some relief for the business pain he had gotten used to and accepted as normal. The analogy worked for him and he signed a contract to work with my client.

When you come across people with suppressed pain, your job is to help them get in touch with their pain so that you can prescribe a cure. Fifty years ago, no one had a copier and they didn't think they would need such a thing. They had carbon paper, low paid secretaries and eventually NCR paper. When Xerox came knocking with their new invention, they had to convince companies that they were in pain, but office staff had been walking with a limp for so long they didn't feel it anymore. Such is the case with many of your potential clients.

Often, potential buyers are not looking for long-term solutions, simply because they don't think a reasonable one exists. Twenty years ago, the "telecopier" was the only way to get a document across the country in a single day. The process was lengthy and expensive, but it was the only option. Then, when the fax machine showed up, all a salesman had to do was put a prospect in touch with his suppressed pain and show him a reasonable solution. Once it existed, pain became evident.

If a salesman is experienced and has a good knowledge of his product, he can most likely spot the needs of potential buyers, but a common mistake is to present a solution that the prospects aren't looking for. Resist the temptation to prescribe a solution until you have developed their "suppressed pain" into "admitted pain" through questioning. Don't tell the clients how much pain they are in. Get them to admit the pain. They will believe their own words well before they will believe yours. In short, never tell customers something you can ask them!

Admitted pain, seeking a plan

This is where buyers have a pain, will admit it, but don't know how to solve it. They are unhappy with the current situation and are actively seeking a workable solution. Once buyers admit pain, the most common mistake is to prescribe a solution before doing an in-depth diagnosis. This is similar to a patient telling a doctor he's having stomach pains and the doctor prescribing a medication to coat the stomach only to find out later that the pain was caused by stomach cancer, requiring a much different treatment.

Before you prescribe a solution, listen to the symptoms. Ask a lot of questions. You may only be seeing the tip of the iceberg, so don't assume that you or your prospects fully understand the pain. Also, don't assume that your prospects know the cure. Draw the pain out of them. Don't prescribe until you agree on the cause of the pain and course of treatment.

Have pain, have plan

This is where buyers recognize their pain, have determined its cause and have a plan to correct it. Typically, their plan has been developed by the last doctor (competitor) to call on their business. The scenario looks something like this: "Bill, we're getting bids on repair work needed on two of our transformers with leaky bushings and we want to clean the oil as well. To match apples with apples, I'd like you to bid on the cost using a filter press like XYZ Company has suggested." Typically, buyers in this mode know who will be taking what action when and with which supplier and product.

All too often when buyers are saying, "I need it," the seller responds with, "I've got it," when in fact the best solution for customers may be an entirely different process than the one the competitor has recommended. You might make the sale based on price by matching his bid requirements, but you won't develop customer loyalty in the process. A doctor who gives an unknown man a painkiller for his back, simply because he requested it, without asking any questions or giving an examination is not building patient loyalty. As the seller, you should diagnose the situation yourself. Ask the P-A-I-N index questions. Walk buyers through their problem (P), assess cause and effect (A), explore the implications (I) and agree on the vision of what's next (N). It's critical that you and your customers jointly participate in the vision of what's next.

Understanding the need

First understand, then be understood

St. Francis of Assisi in the early thirteenth century was the one who said we ought to first understand, then be understood, but his wisdom has gone unheeded. Make a point of trying to understand your customers' needs, priorities, worldview, circumstances, preferences, etc. Only when you have a proper understanding of their specific need can you begin to truly help them with your solution. I once had a young boy in Central America try to convince me that my white Reebok's needed shining. He was trying to make me understand that he could shine my shoes before determining if I was a good candidate for his services. Salespeople do this on a daily basis.

Fully meet a buyer's need and your need will be fully met

Zig Ziglar says that if you help enough people get what they want, you will eventually get what you want. In sales, I succeed by making my clients' need, my need. I take the burden of solving their problem as if it was my burden and I go to work on solving it. In essence, this is the Golden Rule of selling. If I was the buyer, I would want someone who understands my pain thoroughly to come alongside and help me find lasting relief to my pain as quickly and economically as possible. Make a point of learning your customers' goals, then treat their goals like they are your own and help your customers reach those goals. In the process your needs will be fully met. Remember, we succeed when we help others reach their goals, not ours.

Find a need and explore the far-reaching consequences

It's not enough to learn of a need. You must learn the full impact of that need in terms of economic impact, job security, production schedules, personal comfort, etc. In short, find out why it matters. Your job as you walk customers through the PAIN questions is to uncover the monster that harasses or terrorizes them, and then slay it. Don't slay it before they acknowledge its existence or they won't be impressed!

Nobody needs your product!

People don't need your product; they need the *product of your product.* For example, several years ago I had written a book that I thought bookstores would be sure to carry, but when I called, they quickly informed me that they already had plenty of books in their stores. There was no shortage of book publishers offering to put books on their shelves. What they needed were the profits that a book could provide. In order to sell bookstores on my books, I had to show them how they could profit more from stocking my books than someone else's.

Likewise, the end-users who would be purchasing my books from the store didn't wake up one morning and tell themselves they needed another book to put on their shelves at home. My book had to communicate that it could meet a need in a clear, concise and compelling manner. In your line of work, remember that nobody wants your product; they want the prestige, service, revenue, or whatever benefits your product provides. So, help them see the product of your product.

Remember that your customers are people. Your customers are not hospitals, churches, large industrial plants, or restaurants. Your customers are people who may work in those environments, but they are first of all people. If you will simply make their needs your needs and show them how you can satisfy those needs better than anyone else can show them, you will win their business. Notice, I didn't say you had to have a better product than everyone else does, you just have to be able to articulate the need and your solution better than your competition.

7

The Art of
Gaining Rapport

Rapport is a sympathetic connection between people. It involves the heart and soul in the sales process and is very important to establish as early on as possible. Establishing rapport with people means winning their hearts and having them emotionally on your side. The mind will justify what the heart wants. In order to win the battle for their hearts, you must first demonstrate that you care. As the old adage says, "People don't care how much you know, until they know how much you care."

Rapport rule
1

Talk is cheap

Nearly everyone promises great service, great pricing and the best value. When was the last time you heard a salesman tell you that his product was overpriced, mediocre in quality, and that his service policy was marginal at best? Salesmen won't say that, but you do need to clearly differentiate yourself from the competition. How can you show your customers that your words are authentic? Simple—you serve from the heart to win the heart.

For example, a friend of mine was buying a fax machine for his office. He called two companies for recommendations. The first one sent him a brochure expounding on the benefits of his product line and the service of his company. The second salesman was from a smaller firm and instead of telling my friend about their company's great service, he began delivering that service from the beginning. He brought out a fax machine for him to see, touch and even use. His price was actually a little higher, but because he had already begun servicing him so well, my friend bought from him—at the higher price. You don't merely tell prospects that you care and that you will look after them in the future, you must show them that you care now, before you get the order.

Rapport rule
2

All things being equal, buyers will purchase from a person they like

Things are rarely equal in a competitive selling situation, but when things are close, buyers will usually lean towards the person who has done the best job of developing rapport. Some companies recognize this and spend significant sums of money to "win" buyers, often crossing an ethical line in the process. Typically, companies rely too much on this strategy. I was consulting with a company whose entire sales strategy consisted of the "good ol' boy" strategy. They believed that if they were nice enough, for long enough, buying enough meals and doing enough favors, they would eventually get the business. Although this had some positive effect, as a stand-alone strategy, it failed. Developing rapport with customers can give you a powerful advantage, but don't put all your eggs in that basket. Sometimes you may be secure in the rapport you've developed with a purchasing agent only to find your competitor has made an economically compelling case to the president of the company.

Rapport rule
3

To win a buyer's friendly and favorable disposition, show yourself friendly and give favor

People like people who make them feel good. When people feel good about things, they are less afraid to part with their money. Part of your job is to put people at ease. Make them feel comfortable with you and the entire selling process. Let them know you understand this may be a big or a difficult decision for them and that you will endeavor to help them come to the best possible outcome.

Rapport rule
4

The mind justifies what the heart desires

Many years ago I needed another vehicle. Reliable transportation would have been fine, but I found myself wanting a recent model Mercedes. My heart was tugging one way and my mind was being far more practical. In the end, my heart won and my mind provided the justification. I reasoned that the Mercedes would be good for hundreds of thousands of miles with little maintenance. With the amount of travel I did, having a reliable car made sense and I rationalized that it would cost less in the end because of its life expectancy and strong resale value. The sale was made in my heart and justified in my mind. So it is with most sales. In fact, many experts agree that ninety percent of the decision is made in the heart and only ten percent with intellectual reasoning. Most people would rather reason out what their heart wants than submit their heart to what their mind says is best.

The heart is the real battleground, and in a competitive environment, you won't have great success without winning the battle for the heart. The mind, however, is the negotiating table. You need to be prepared to provide the kind of logical justification the buyer needs to make himself—or his boss who isn't emotionally involved—feel better about the purchase.

To win the battle for the heart, you need to secure confidence in three things:

1. You:

If customers don't feel good about you as a person, you will have a difficult time winning them over on anything else you have to say. Help customers out by being on time, showing respect, honoring them, etc.

2. Your product or service:

Customers may feel good about you, but if they don't feel good about what you have to offer, your sale is lost.

3. Your company:

Customers may like you and your product, but if they have strong reservations about your company, you may still lose the sale. The battle for the heart is waged on three fronts, and you must be prepared to compete and win in all three.

Seven areas of conflict you may encounter in the battle for the heart

We are three-part beings, comprised of spirit, soul and body. When people surrender their lives to Christ, their spirits are born again. Their souls, however, consisting of the mind, will and emotions, are in need of a lot of regeneration.

Around 1400 BC, the Israelite nation was about to take over a land inhabited principally by seven hostile tribes that God wanted driven out. Each of these tribal names have meanings that relate to a negative character trait commonly found among people today. They were the Hittites, Girgashites, Amorites, Canaanites, Perizzites, Hivites and the Jebusites, and they were stronger than the Israelites. The decisive factor wasn't who was strongest, but rather, whose side God was on.

Kill 'em with kindness
— the Hittite Conflict

Hittite means "hostile," and admittedly, there are a lot of people who have a hostile nature. They carry anger just below the surface and it doesn't take much to get on their wrong side. A common trait of those who carry inner hostility is intimidation. They attempt to get what they want through intimidation, be that a price concession, a better delivery date, or a free upgrade.

This happened to me. Early in my sales career, I called on a new company to see about selling them a copier. I began to ask the receptionist a few qualifying questions to see if it was worthwhile to set an appointment with a buyer. As I was standing there, the owner strutted by and in a deep guttural voice said, "Get rid of him!" I was both intimidated and angry. I started backing out asking questions in my retreat (much like you might imagine Columbo would have done in his television role as a detective). Before I was finished, he walked by again and in a much angrier, more hostile tone barked, "I said, 'Get rid of him!'" It was just about quitting time and as soon as he walked away, the receptionist grabbed her coat and ran out of the office leaving me still standing there in the reception area.

Instead of leaving as well, I decided to respond in the opposite spirit. I walked into the office area and found the owner standing in the hallway speaking with some of his executives. I walked right up to him and introduced myself as if nothing had even happened and responded with outer confidence (I was trembling on the inside), deciding to "kill 'em with kindness." This is the "a soft answer turns away wrath" principle from Proverbs 15:1. To my amazement, it worked. He arranged a meeting with his controller, which ultimately led to a purchase.

Demonstrate loyalty, emphasize value & think long-term
—the Girgashite Conflict

Girgashite means "clay dweller" or "one who turns back from a pilgrimage." A common attribute of people with this characteristic is disloyalty. They tend to break promises and reveal confidences. Be careful what you reveal to them, because they may share it with your competition. Nonetheless, with every customer including them you must: demonstrate loyalty, establish a good relationship, keep your promises, deliver what you promise by when you promised, be trustworthy, and help them see the long-term value in your proposition. Disloyal people are prone to turn away from you with just the slightest provocation. Model for them true commitment and help them to feel secure with you because they need to see that turning back from you is their loss.

Be positive. Find areas of agreement
—the Amorite Conflict

Amorite means "critical." A common characteristic of critical buyers is their faultfinding, negative attitude towards you, your product, your company, your profession, and life in general. They can be difficult to deal with, but we are to love our enemies, do good to those who hate us, and pray for those who use us in a despiteful manner (Matthew 5:44).

Back when I was selling copiers, my boss met me for lunch one day in my territory. I arrived at the restaurant a little early, so I decided to make a cold prospect call on the large multinational company next door. I walked in the reception area and asked to speak with the purchasing agent. To my delight, she agreed to meet me in the lobby. When she approached me she said, "The only reason I came down here was to tell you to your face that I don't ever want you or anyone from your company in our office again. We have several of your copiers upstairs and they've been nothing but trouble. When the lease expires in three months, we're getting all new equipment from your competitor. We have one of their copiers downstairs and have had no troubles for five years with it. I know you're new with the company, but when you see your boss, tell him that I hate him!" She put a whole new chill on the term, "cold calling!"

I walked back to the restaurant to await my boss. Though my heart was beating fast, my mind tried to remain calm. I realized that when customers are really angry with you or your firm, there is still hope, but when they become complacent or indifferent, the challenge to win their loyalty increases exponentially. This is like a wife yelling at her husband, "I hate you!" The strong show of negative emotion is an indication that there was a significant deposit of positive emotion that has suffered loss. If there was a prior deposit of positive emotion, the husband has a good chance in taking responsibility for his action that caused the loss, then rebuilding on the significant reasons that led to there being a deposit of positive emotions in the first place. However, if the wife wakes up one morning and calmly states, "I don't love you anymore," the marriage is in deep trouble. Similarly, when your customers express anger at you or your company for poor performance, don't run and hide. Take responsibility head on and watch how quickly you can win back their loyalty.

When my boss arrived a few minutes later, I told him about my cold call and the fact that the purchasing agent hated him. He explained that she had every right to feel the way she did and that the company had truly dropped the ball with them. In fact, it was such a fiasco that nobody wanted to go in there. He said, "I'll tell you what I'm going to do. I'm going to give you this account. It will be all yours to see what you can do with it." Can you imagine my gratitude? I had enough problems getting started in a new territory without taking this one on, except for one thing: she had said that they were getting all new equipment in three months. I reasoned that anyone that unhappy, at one time, had high expectations with our company, so I accepted the challenge.

The first thing I did was to put her name on a 3x5 card along with certain relevant facts about her company and carried it in my shirt pocket. Each morning on the way to work I would pray for her. If she could treat a total stranger with such contempt, she needed to experience some of God's love, so I prayed daily that God would show her how much He loved her. After awhile, I had an idea and had a technician call her to propose removing her equipment for the purpose of "refurbishing" it so that the last three months of service would be better. We offered to loan her all new equipment free of charge while we refurbished the old copiers.

She agreed and the exchange took place.

Suddenly, all the employees wanted to keep the new equipment, so she requested a bid from me and some of my competitors. In the meantime, I showed empathy, agreed with the premise of her dissatisfaction, and we eventually came to an agreement for a satisfactory remedy of the problem. My kindness, compassion and positive outlook paid off, because by the time the process was over, the seemingly insurmountable credibility deficit was overcome and she decided to purchase our copiers instead of our competitor's. In fact, it was the largest commercial order our company got that year!

To top it all off, she asked me to arrange a meeting between her and my boss, the very guy she hated so much. When he went to her office, she apologized for her attitude towards him and asked him to forgive her. Talk about a complete turnaround! A kind response on our part definitely turned away her wrath and gave us favor in her eyes.

Exemplify integrity & provide face-saving opportunities
—the Canaanite Conflict

Canaanite means, "traveling merchant." Traveling merchants in those days weren't known for their integrity. Buyers with this trait have a disregard for the truth, misrepresent their needs, withhold pertinent information, and exaggerate the competitor's offer.

Don't play their game. Don't be intimidated and don't compromise. Be firm, show integrity and provide face-saving opportunities where necessary. People don't like to get caught in a lie. If you catch buyers in a lie, it's best not to call them on it directly, but let it be seen, and then let it go. If you embarrass a buyer, you are probably finished with that account for good. You can win in this situation without playing deceptive negotiating games. In the end analysis, if you have shown yourself to be a person of impeccable integrity, you're much more likely to win the sale.

Shift emphasis from price to value
—the Perizzite Conflict

Perizzite means, "unwalled villages." The evident character trait is the desire not to want any boundaries. Such people are selfish, and want what they want when they want it. Typically, they are rude and approach negotiations with a Win/Lose attitude. They will try to beat you down on price and take as much from you as they can get. They have a field day with weaker, untrained sales reps. This strategy will come back to haunt them, especially if their vendor can no longer stay in business to support the purchase they made.

Your job is to shift the emphasis from price to value and convince the prospects of the mutual benefit of a Win/Win negotiation. Approach buyers with a spirit of generosity, but not until you recognize the most generous thing you can do for them is to have them pay a fair price with an appropriate profit so you will be around to serve their long-term needs. Until you recognize the benefits for everyone in a Win/Win outcome and can articulate that convincingly, you will probably find yourself on the losing end of the deal. Remember that there is hardly anything in the world that someone cannot make a little worse and sell a little cheaper. By focusing only on price, you are allowing such buyers to eat you for lunch.

Demonstrate humility.
Ask questions. Listen.
—the Hivite Conflict

Hivite means "serpent" and is characterized by pride. Typically, prideful buyers will demonstrate a superior attitude, show little interest in what you are saying, and believe they already know the answer. You can sometimes be helpful by walking in the opposite spirit—humility. This does not mean you are a doormat and allow buyers to walk all over you.

One of the best ways to demonstrate humility is to ask plenty of questions, listen with interest, and take notes where appropriate. Though tempting, if you "fight it out" with your own prideful responses and win the argument, you will not likely win the sale. Instead, approach these type of people in meekness (strength under control) and let God take care of the "who's right, who's wrong" issue.

Exude confidence. Serve.
Create a positive expectation
—the Jebusite Conflict

Jebusite means, "trodden down" and is typical of people filled with fear. Fearful buyers are typically distrustful and indecisive. You must show empathy and let them know you understand how difficult an important decision can be. Exude confidence with the buyer, because nothing breeds confidence better than confidence. If the doctor performing surgery on you is visibly nervous, how confident are you? But if you are nervous and the doctor walks in with an air that says he's done this a thousand times before and he always has a good result, don't you pick up some of that same confidence? This is also true in sales. Let customers see how confident you are in your recommendations and your vision for their brighter future. Help them see a positive future with your product or service and serve them by removing any areas of ambiguity or uncertainty.

The bottom line to these seven characteristics that you will encounter in the battle for the heart is that they will continue to produce after their own kind. You must be careful not to let buyers plant seeds of criticism, pride, or disloyalty in the field of your heart. Instead, you should plant loyalty, humility, integrity, selflessness, confidence, and kindness. In short, operate in the opposite spirit and watch the seeds of what you plant bring about a bountiful harvest in your customers' lives.

8

Preparing to Give
and Receive Respect

Respect is a two-way street. You must both give it and earn it. If you win a buyer's heart and trust and then it is discovered that you really don't know what you are talking about—that you're ignorant of pertinent information essential to the sale—you stand a good chance of losing the buyer's respect and the sale.

Rule of respect #1 — *Respect brings favor*

Respect fosters trust. If you know that the doctor seeing you for your illness has won a Nobel

Prize for his research in that same field, wouldn't that enhance your respect for him and therefore your trust? In sales, when buyers see something in you they can respect, you will find favor with them. In addition, if you show extra respect to people, you will most likely gain their favor. I heard of a speaker passing his old dusty violin around the room. He let the audience hold it, and with polite interest, they looked at it as they passed it around. When he mention that it was an original Stradivarius worth an estimated $60,000, the audience suddenly paid extra attention and respect to the old violin, all because they recognized its value. People are worth far more than any violin, and looking at them through God's eyes will change how we do business. Imagine treating them with dignity and honor regardless of whether or not anyone else recognizes their value. Imagine how they would respond. Respect and honor do indeed bring favor.

Rule of respect #2 — *To respect means to honor*

When people feel honored, they are much more likely to do business with you. It's easy to understand the effect of dishonoring someone in business, but few of us take time to consider the ways in which we can deliberately honor our prospective customers. A few examples would be to keep your word, arrive on time, be courteous, listen with interest, and give them eye contact. Showing honor or respect to your customer is easier than earning it from your customer. Here are seven ways you can win the respect, honor, esteem and admiration of others:

1. Honor them: You dishonor customers every time you attempt some sort of "cheap close" on them, and you will reap the same in return. I don't like it when a sales rep tries to manipulate me anymore than you like it being done to you, so why would we expect our customers to feel any differently? Honor them with the same honor and respect you would hope for and it will return substantial dividends to you.

"As you would men should do to you, do also to them likewise" (Luke 6:31).

2. Exude confidence: Confidence is a powerful and contagious force. I saw this demonstrated in an illegitimate way by a con man. He went to Yankee stadium to see if he could get in the ball game without having to purchase a ticket. He stood with his face to the wall and told himself over and over again that he owned Yankee stadium and therefore didn't have to buy a ticket like everyone else. Once this was in his spirit, he got in the ticket line, and when it was his turn to buy a ticket, he just stared quietly at the sales clerk with the inner attitude that he owned the stadium and didn't have to pay. She let him pass!

Now all he had to do was hand over the ticket he didn't purchase to the security guard who was ripping the tickets in half as people came through the gate. He did exactly the same thing with the security guard, saying nothing but looking at him with the attitude that he owned the place and nobody better challenge his right to enter the ballpark without paying. The guard let him through without saying a word. His confidence game worked. He went on to use the same technique to enter the press booth where he watched the game in air-conditioned comfort.

The point is that people are more likely to respect you when you exude confidence. We, as Christians, have every reason to be full of confidence.

"Being confident of this very thing that He which hath begun a good work in you will be faithful to complete it until the day of Jesus Christ" (Philippians 1:6).

3. Be knowledgeable: Make yourself a knowledgeable resource to your customers and you will find favor with them. Know more about your field than your customers or your competitors do. In times of difficulty, customers want a reliable, knowledgeable resource and are usually willing to pay extra for it.

"Good understanding brings favor" (Proverbs 13:15).

4. Show mercy: Showing mercy in sales is not attempting to sell something to customers that they don't need, don't want, or can't afford. Just because you can get a sale does not mean you should. You might have a stronger personality and be able to strong-arm someone into buying your product or service, but that doesn't mean you've done the right thing. God promised that when you have mercy and truth, you would find favor and good understanding, not only in man's eyes, but also in His (Proverbs 3:4). We need the favor of God working for us in the marketplace!

Not too long ago the 75th anniversary edition of *Sales and Marketing Management* magazine described the near fatal free-fall of IBM stock when it lost seventy percent of its value, forcing the company to eliminate about 40,000 sales and sales-related positions. A former salesman was quoted saying, "We were so well-trained, we could sell anything, good or bad. So under quota pressures, we sold systems that our customers didn't need, didn't want and couldn't afford." The short-term gains were eclipsed by the near-fatal long-term loss.

"Let not mercy and truth forsake you..." *(Proverbs 3:3).*

5. Be truthful: The joke, "How do you know when a salesman is lying? His lips are moving!" is well deserved because the sales industry has earned the reputation. People are more likely to respect someone who tells them of the product's weaknesses than they will the one that denies the product has any weaknesses. It's not enough to tell the truth. You need to develop the policy of practicing full disclosure. Make sure the customers understand all the facts that would influence their decision. I used to sell a liquid-toner, plain paper copier that was highly reliable but performed poorly when copying on to certain absorbent letterhead stocks. Customers would occasionally ask if the copier could copy on letterhead. The truth was that it could, but the whole truth was that the copy quality would vary greatly depending on the paper stock. In my line of work, not every salesman felt compelled to reveal the whole truth.

In addition to telling the whole truth, sales reps need to take ownership of the responsibility of making sure the customers actually hear and understand the whole truth. Sometimes you can reveal a weakness of your product and you know it went right over your prospects' heads. If you don't make sure they really do know and understand the whole truth, it can come back to bite you later. Tell the whole truth and earn your customers' respect in the process.

"Let not mercy and truth forsake you..." (Proverbs 3:3).

6. Possess wisdom: There was once a man who ran several businesses in addition to holding public office and having a consulting practice on the side. He was big into thoroughbred horses and land development. He was so successful that people came from all over to glean from his wisdom. He was so confident in the value of his wisdom that he let the customers set the price, paying only what they thought it was worth. In one year, his international consulting clients and local patrons paid him approximately $280 million in gold bullion! That doesn't count the money he made in his other business enterprises. His name was Solomon. He was famous for his pursuit, acquisition and dispersal of priceless wisdom, much of which was recorded in Proverbs. When you possess real wisdom, the marketplace will make room for you and honor you with trust, respect and substance.

"Exalt wisdom and she will promote you. She will bring you to honor when you embrace her" (Proverbs 4:8).

7. Promise well – deliver more than well: In this highly competitive age, it's difficult to promise small and deliver big because there's always someone who will promise big and make your promise look insignificant. By the time they deliver small and disappoint the customer, it's too late for you, and for the customer. So you should promise as big as you know you can deliver, then go the extra mile and deliver a little more. That will win the initial battle for your customers and keep them coming back for more. Always hold yourself responsible for a higher standard than anybody else expects of you, and never excuse yourself.

"He that diligently seeks good finds favor" (Proverbs 11:27).

Rule of respect #3 — *Responsibility precedes authority*

When you demonstrate that you are responsible for the words you speak (doing what you say you will do), you are on your way to gaining authority over a portion of your customers' resources. If you can demonstrate that you are reliable and can be counted on, your customers are much more likely to sign over the sum of money to your authority so they can acquire from you the product or service you are offering. Too often in sales a sales rep asks for the resources before he has demonstrated responsibility.

The spiritual law is that authority follows responsibility, as Luke 19:17 makes plain: "Because you have been faithful in a very little, have authority over ten cities."

Rule of respect #4 — *The small things are the hardest*

It has been said that by small means, great things are accomplished. I used to think that the small things were the easy part, but I've come to believe that the small things are the most difficult. In sales, small things may include sending a "Thank You" card, returning a call promptly, delivering a sample in a timely manner or preparing a written quote instead of providing a verbal quote. Small things include activities such as good record keeping, timely follow-up, and even daily sales reports. When you do the small things well, you are much better prepared to accept the responsibility of handling the big things.

Rule of respect #5 — *Don't despise the small things*

A lot of sales reps despise small things, always chasing the big sale, and are never willing to do the small daily things that will take them there with more certainty. When I sold copiers, my boss insisted that all the salesmen fill out daily reports of all their sales activities. Everyone hated this task and most did it only under threat of holding back car allowance checks. I didn't like completing them either, but I did them faithfully every day and turned them in weekly. I never saw him ever read the reports. After four years I was still the youngest and most inexperienced man on the team, but he asked me to accept the position of sales manager. He told me that I was the only one who was willing to be under authority and was therefore the only one who was ready to be in authority. I became the youngest sales manager in their history and had a successful term in that position before starting a business of my own. Don't despise the small things. Do them as unto the Lord and He will reward you in due time.

9

Building a Bridge
of Trust

Trust is the drawbridge over which you transport your product or service into the lives of your prospects. Without trust, it is very difficult to accomplish this because trust is the highest form of human motivation. If I need a car and my uncle Bob is a car salesman, but I don't trust him, then I'm not likely to do business with him. My mountain of respect for his knowledge of automobiles does nothing to alter the fact that I don't trust him. It is critically important to lay a foundation of trust and keep building on that throughout the selling process. Trust makes us feel secure and when we feel secure, we relax our grip on our pocketbook.

Trust bridge 1 — *Trust is subjective when your track record is not known*

Until your customers have facts to base their opinions on, they have little more than subjective feelings or impressions to guide them in their evaluation of you. On a business trip in Dallas many years ago, my wife and I met with a businessman who had come highly recommended. After our first meeting, my wife plainly stated that she didn't trust him. I was shocked and quickly reminded her of his high credentials. She had no "concrete" reason for her feelings, apart from the way he avoided eye contact. Foolishly, I dismissed her warning and continued pursuing the relationship. At the last minute the deal fell through, and it was a good thing too! I narrowly missed a shipwreck, but it wasn't without its share of difficulty.

The fact of the matter is that people evaluate us initially on a purely subjective level, "reading" us based by what we project. If you have improper intent, your customers may not be able to figure out exactly why they feel that way, but they may very well feel "uncomfortable" with you. The best way to make a positive first impression on someone is to possess a high degree of personal integrity. It will exude from you and people will sense it.

Trust bridge 2 — *Preconceived ideas can significantly impact trust levels*

We already know that being a salesman is often equated with being a liar, but more and more sales reps are viewing buyers as liars as well.

Neither position is accurate, despite what we have experienced. These preconceived ideas enter into the buying and selling process. Recognize where your customers are along the trust continuum and meet them there, then help them move at their pace along the continuum until trust is high.

Trust bridge 3 — *High-trust questions before low-trust answers increase buyer resistance*

When customers walk into your piano store and are interested in purchasing a baby grand piano, do you ask them what their annual income is before you begin showing them the piano? You might, but if you ask before you've earned the right to ask for sensitive information, you may be shooting yourself in the foot. There's a trust-building cycle that looks something like this:

1. You provide low-trust information (name, purpose of call, etc.).
2. Buyer agrees to meet with you.
3. You ask low-trust questions (circumstantial about company and process).
4. Buyer gives you low-trust answers.
5. You provide higher-trust information about yourself, company or product.
6. You ask higher-trust questions about needs, pains, budget, etc.
7. Buyer gives you higher-trust answers.

As mutual trust increases, the drawbridge lowers.

Trust bridge 4 — *Personal trustworthiness precedes public trust*

People who are not trustworthy will not gain and keep trust for long. Early in my sales career I once lost a sale to a much more experienced sales rep from a prestigious and well-known competitive company. A week after I lost the sale, the accountant called me and said he had just canceled his contract due to a blatant misrepresentation by the salesman and he wanted to purchase my equipment and take delivery immediately. When I arrived to formalize our agreement, he told me that he realized I was "too naive to lie" and he should have done business with me in the first place. Well, as a young and struggling sales rep, I had found something that the marketplace valued more than slick presentations or powerful closing techniques—trustworthiness. I began to build my career on that revelation.

Trust bridge 5 — *It's hard to get someone to trust you more than you trust them*

In sales you have to take chances and be willing to trust others before they trust you. Trust begets trust and suspicion begets suspicion. A few years ago I was helping a friend purchase a quality used automobile. He selected a model he was interested in and the salesman pulled out his pricing binder, laid it on the hood of the car and began looking for the price. As he moved his finger down the page, I stepped over to his side to see the pricing along with him. To my surprise, he grabbed the pricing binder and pulled it to his chest, denying me the information it contained. What trust I had in him instantly disappeared! When he didn't trust me with the full pricing information, I naturally didn't trust him to take my friend's money for the car or any other car at the dealership. We went elsewhere to find someone we could trust and bought a car there.

On the flip side, when I was just about eight-years old, I embarked on a short-lived life of crime. It all began with what I thought was a well planned shoplifting heist estimated to be worth about two cents at the time. I had an accomplice with me who was to be on lookout while I cased the grocery store looking for candy. My plan was a good one, or so I thought. I would slip a couple of packages of penny candy in my winter jacket pocket where I also had about thirteen cents. Then I would make my way to the checkout counter, pick up a ten-cent candy bar and pay for it. If anyone discovered my theft, I would claim that I had just forgotten about the candy in my pocket, that I had every intention of paying for it, and would offer as proof the fact that I paid for the more expensive piece of candy and had sufficient money to pay for the less expensive ones in my pocket.

On my way out of the store, head hanging low, eyes unable to look straight ahead, dripping with guilt, I walked straight into a rather large storekeeper who had seen the whole thing and accused me of shoplifting. Of course, I gave him my pre-planned explanation, but it held no water with him since he had watched me covertly place the candy in my pocket. He called my father who came down to the grocery store to sort the matter out. I knew that life for me was about to end and I only had one chance to save it and that was to perfect that story I had told the storekeeper. When my father arrived, I told him the same story, if for no other reason than to buy myself a few extra minutes of life. I told him my lie, and to my shock and amazement, he turned to the storekeeper and said, "If my son says it's so, then it's so!" He proceeded to lecture him for picking on a kid, and then escorted me safely home.

I had never been more relieved and more ashamed at the same time in my life. Relieved because I was not in trouble, but ashamed because my father actually took my word above the word of an adult and I had betrayed the trust he had bestowed on me. I turned over a new leaf that day, endeavoring to live up to the trust expectation my father had of me. His trust in me encouraged me to rise to that level of trust and to become trustworthy.

Seven ways to create a climate of trust

Knowing that trust is the highest form of human motivation, I have often wondered if there was a reliable model for creating a climate of trust. As I thought about it, I realized that Jesus Christ asks you and me to trust Him for our eternal salvation. So how did He model His life in such a way that we would be reasonably inclined, expected, and even held accountable for our decision to trust or not trust Him? My answer came with the Apostle Paul's summation of the life of Christ in seven very poignant points (Philippians 2:5-8). These seven points are very powerful and are a highly effective business model for creating a climate of trust.

Seven steps to ironclad trust

1. **Be confident**— *"...did not consider it robbery to be equal with God..."*

> Jesus was completely confident in His identity as Son of God and son of man. He didn't think it improper to be considered equal with God because He was fully God. His confidence in the face of His harshest critics silenced their arguments and won the hearts of the common man. When customers sense that you have confidence in the solution you are presenting to them, it builds confidence in them towards your proposition.
>
> When my friend would receive inquiries from people who were shopping the market for the kind of product he sold, he would tell them with great and genuine confidence that their search was over, they could relax now because he was involved, and that he would take care of them. I was always amazed at how these prospects latched onto his confidence and in many cases no longer felt the need to seek out competitive offers.

2. **Be vulnerable**— *"...but made Himself of no reputation..."*

Most people are uncomfortable with the idea of having less of a reputation than they feel they deserve. Vulnerability is weakness, in their eyes, but Jesus stripped Himself of rank and privilege. He could have called down every angel in Heaven to protect Him or He could have instantly blinded every Roman centurion and walked away untouched at the time of His crucifixion. But instead, He made Himself vulnerable. He walked among the common people, lived in their world, and suffered many of their hardships, in the process winning the full and complete trust of those He came to seek and save. Consider a hostage negotiator. When he walks up to where the gunman is holding people hostage, does he walk up armed to the teeth or does he lay his weapons down in plain sight? He lays his weapons down, making himself vulnerable, and in the process wins the trust of the gunman.

In sales, you can be vulnerable by freely admitting your product's weaknesses. When you hide the truth, people can sense it and they will resist you at least at a subconscious level. I would rather buy a used car from someone who would tell me everything that was wrong with it than from someone who tried to make me believe that the car was flawless. There's nothing wrong with admitting weakness in your product. People don't expect any product to be the complete answer to their needs. Of course, you should be well versed with your strengths and be able to show how those offset the weaknesses. If you're new to sales, don't hesitate to tell that to your customers. More than likely they will try to help you make the sale, but if you act like you know everything when you clearly don't, you will lose their confidence and quite likely the sale.

3.   Excel in service— "...*taking on the form of a bondservant...*"

Jesus did not come to be served, but to serve. He had no hidden agenda. He washed His disciples' feet, fed the hungry, healed the sick, gave hope to the broken-hearted and preached tirelessly to the poor and needy. His life of service brought great trust. If you would like to win the trust of people, try taking on the attitude of a servant and give yourself to discovering and serving their real needs. Believe me, you will earn their trust.

General Ephraim Rios Mont, the former president of Guatemala, is one such example. He was an incredibly gracious man who saved his country from a communist takeover back in the eighties. A friend of mine was a pastor in Guatemala and was invited to the presidential palace to meet General Rios Mont. My friend was treated gruffly by the armed security guards and was nervous about meeting the president. He was ushered into a room to wait. The house was fully staffed with servants, but when General Rios Mont came in, he walked over to my friend, knelt before him and offered to get him some tea or coffee. My friend felt very awkward, but accepted the kind offer. A few minutes later, the president returned with the coffee on a tray and again knelt in front of my friend, serving him from a posture of lowly servitude. The president was the most powerful man in the country, but he was also an ardent follower of Jesus Christ and chose to follow Christ's example. The people of Guatemala responded with tremendous favor towards their new president and he is dearly loved to this day.

Excelling in service will create a climate of trust towards you.

4.   Identify with the buyer— *"...and coming in the likeness of men..."*

Look for things in common with your potential customers, and when you find that common ground, build on it.

Several years ago, my wife's son was killed in a car accident. A few months later we were at a trade show for our business and were introduced to the president of a large distribution company. As we chatted in the aisle, he asked my wife how many kids we had. It was the first time that question had been asked since we had buried her nineteen-year-old son. She hesitated for a moment and then fighting back tears, said that she had one in Nashville and one in Heaven, and then she started to cry. Unbeknownst to us, the president had also buried his first-born son and was moved to tears as he recounted his story. I had also buried my first-born child. At that moment, very unexpectedly, the three of us forged a most unusual bond, as only those who have buried their children can understand. When the topic returned to business, the unspoken trust was very high and we quickly formed a business relationship that benefits both of us to this day. We had found some common ground and trust was established at a deep level. On that basis we moved with confidence through all the other negotiations that followed.

5. **Be humble**— "...*And being found in appearance as a man, He humble Himself...*"

It's always easier to trust a humble man than a prideful, arrogant man. At a sales conference, a somewhat nervous salesman stood up to speak. Several very polished, gregarious speakers had just finished dazzling the audience with their humor, wit and charm. The salesman told no funny stories and stayed glued to the podium. He taught a short session, telling about his own failures and how he found faith in God.

When he was finished his somewhat monotone talk, he received a raving, standing ovation, the only one given that day. He reportedly earned millions of dollars in annual sales commissions, certainly more earning power than those he shared the stage with, but he had an unmistakable attitude of humility. Even though he had more to boast about than any other speaker, he boasted only in his weakness and quietly shared his secrets for success. No doubt his authentic humility engendered trust with his clients and contributed to his remarkable success. His talk was also the only one I remembered.

6. Possess personal integrity even when it hurts— *"and became obedient to the point of death..."*

When you go the extra mile for a customer, even when it costs you, it builds trust in a way that nothing else can. Sometimes you have to lose money on a sale to keep your integrity in tact. At an international seminar for about 250 people, I discovered only a few days before the event that my advertisement had been "edited" to say that lunch was provided, but the ad I approved earlier had clearly stated that lunch was not provided. The ads were wrong, the budget did not include lunch, but the people were expecting it! So I bought 250 people lunch at a rather nice hotel downtown. It was either that or try to explain during my seminar on Biblical principles for business why I was violating what I was teaching. There was no other choice, even though it hurt.

7. Trade places— *"...even the death of the cross."*

We need to put ourselves in our customers' place, empathizing with them and carrying their burdens as our own. My father once spent two days talking a man out of purchasing about $150,000 worth of bowling alley equipment because it wasn't in the man's best interest and my father knew the man would go broke if the deal went through. Sure, it cost him the sale, but that kind of integrity kept my dad consistently in the number one sales position in the company. By putting yourself in their shoes, you can see more clearly the right decision to make.

10

Making Value Propositions & Interest Statements

It's been said that more than 75% of jurors decide about the guilt or innocence of the accused by the end of the opening statements and don't change their minds throughout the trial! In sales, the start you get in a sales call can have a tremendous impact on the outcome.

Typically, your goal is to attract the initial interest of your prospect in order to win the right to advance to the next step, such as an in-depth interview or needs assessment. At the very least, you are earning the right to proceed with your questioning.

Frequently I ask business owners, sales reps, or managers for their value proposition by asking, "What is it that you bring to the table that differentiates you from your competition in a way that clearly demonstrates value, and can you articulate that in a clear, concise, emotionally compelling and unmatched manner?" Most companies have a value proposition, but most haven't taken the time to think it through, much less learn how to articulate it well. Many times they think that their business is so similar to the competition that it's difficult to differentiate between the two. Compelling value propositions that excite both the sales force and the customers are needed.

Every one of us, whether we own the business or not, have to ask ourselves what makes us different from our competition. In sales training, everyone promises to increase sales, so I have to know what makes me different. There are many different styles and systems for bringing increase in sales, so I have to focus on the unique aspects of my program. I know it will be of high value to some clients and of less value to others because it is simply impossible to be all things to all people.

If you work for a company that has no clarified value proposition and no interest in clarifying anything, it is still in your best interest to think like the owner and ask yourself, "What is it about me and my company, product, or service that differentiates me in a positive, value enhancing way?" Think it through and practice it on others and in the marketplace until you've got it down. When you have refined it, use it with every customer. Find a way to incorporate it into every written message that you write and every presentation that you make.

Four tips to make a lasting impression with a potential customer:

Tip 1 —   There is no second chance for a first impression

Whether you like it or not, people size you up from the moment they see you. They judge the way you dress, whether your shoes are scuffed or shined, whether you came prepared or unprepared, which words you use, your eye contact, your handshake, etc. So do your best to make the first impression a good impression.

Tip 2 —   The first five to six seconds set the tone

This is where you've got to get the customer on track with you. If you're calling on the phone, be sure to introduce your company first, then yourself, followed by your compelling value proposition and the reason for your call. Suppose you're a publisher calling on bookstores; your call might go something like this: "Mr. Jones? Mr. Jones, I'm calling from Northern Publishing. My name is Tim Johnson. Our company specializes in publishing historical narratives of people and events that shaped the landscape of history with a Christian worldview. The reason I called Mr. Jones is that we have our best selling trilogy on the American Revolution packaged in a special Fourth of July counter display that is selling extremely well at bookstores like yours across the country. If you have a moment, I would like to tell you about our special 50% discount and extended terms for this popular Fourth of July special."

You succeeded in identifying yourself and your company, along with what makes your publishing company different from the many thousands that are out there. You also made the reason for your call clear and gave the highlights of your promotional offer before asking for permission to proceed further. This is important because if you had called and just identified yourself and your company, then asked for a few minutes to talk without giving a good reason up-front, the bookstore owner would likely deny your request.

So identify yourself and your company, give your value proposition, the reason for your call and any highlight that would give the individual a reason to want to keep listening. This kind of approach requires a lot of forethought, not extemporaneous speaking. Take the time to script out your initial call, and if you are calling in person, commit your opening remarks to memory.

Tip 3 —   The first three minutes establish the level of effectiveness in your communication

If the customer gives you the go-ahead to continue, you need to have your next step clearly planned in your mind. When the customer senses you have a solid direction you're taking the interview, it will put them at ease, but if they sense that you're floundering, they will end the call for you.

Tip 4 —   Make your opening moments of interest and importance to the prospect

With so much at stake at the beginning of your call and people so hasty to make a decision, don't you think it is well worth the investment of time to carefully and thoughtfully plan out and rehearse your opening remarks? This does not mean that you read them over the phone, but it does mean that you must become so familiar with where you want to take the customers that you can deliver your opening remarks with interest and importance, causing the customers to value what they hear enough to give you permission to continue the call.

11
The Importance of Good Questions

It has been said that we have two ears and one mouth for a reason. I believe one of the reasons that so many in sales do most of the talking is because that's how they've been trained. They get weeks of product training to learn about what their company has to offer, sometimes followed up with skill training on how to close a sale and perhaps even some good old fashioned motivational speaking. But how often does a sales rep get good training on how to listen and what to listen for?

If you're going to listen to customers, then you'll have to learn to ask questions—good questions. Sales are made based on what the customer says, not on what you say. Questions unlock motivation, motivation reveals need, and need is the basis for acquisition. In sales, it's your job to help customers see how your product, service or idea meets their need better than other (available) options. There's no better starting point than with good questions.

My first sales job was selling life insurance. I was taught to knock on someone's door and begin talking a mile-a-minute with my canned presentation as soon as the door opened. I was so scared I didn't even look at the prospect, let alone ask them any questions about their needs. I thought I was there to sell them something, which I thought could only be done by telling them something. I didn't realize that selling was a process that you walk through *with* the buyer, not something you do *to* the buyer.

Eventually I learned to ask questions and find out about them, but there was no rhyme or reason to my approach. Many of the questions I asked were about the latest sporting event, the weather, or the trophy on their shelf, all of which can be fine for ice breakers but take you no where strategically in advancing the sale and helping the customer. I desperately needed a sound approach and found one in God's Word. I had noticed how often Jesus asked questions to uncover motivation, determine need and overcome objections. I could see the power of good questioning and began searching the Scriptures for a model.

Let's be honest, who are you more likely to believe, a total stranger making fantastic claims about some product or your own claims based upon your discovery of the facts? Obviously, you'll always believe your own conclusions faster than those offered by someone else, especially a stranger with a profit motive. But many in the sales profession find themselves in the position of being the stranger calling on a prospective customer with the hopes of making a sale, and thus having a profit motive. How can the prospective customer be put at ease? The answer is to lead the customer through the process of discovery with well thought out questions. As customers answer the questions, they will believe their own answers and be far more comfortable in doing business with you.

Never force-feed customers facts and features they aren't hungry for. Always lead them to the point of discovery by making them thirst for your solutions. You've heard it said, "You can lead a horse to water, but you can't make him drink." Well, if you give the horse salt, you won't be able to stop him from drinking. And in sales, questions are the salt that makes customers want to acquire your product. Remember that sales are made based on what customers say, not on what the salesman says. Therefore, to succeed in sales, you must learn the art of questioning.

This principle of asking questions is effective in any profession. The four critical characteristics of good questions are in the following acronym:

S   Simple

A   Aimed

L   Leading

T   Timely

Simple

When I think of simple questions, I think of the two questions that God asked Adam and Eve: "Where are you?" and "Who told you that you were naked?" These questions stripped away pretension, exposed motivation and uncovered need. When you go into the marketplace to offer your ideas, prepare your listeners with well thought out, simple, penetrating questions that cut to the core of the issues, expose motivation and reveal need.

Whether that need be a product, service, or idea, you need to lead listeners to the solution with questions that are not hard to understand or grasp. You don't want to intimidate your customers or make them feel inferior. Instead, make listeners feel valued and at ease.

The necessary forethought will require a deep understanding of the intrinsic value of your offering and an equally insightful understanding of human need and how that need relates to your product or service. Simple questions should never mean a lack of intelligent forethought that takes into consideration (and anticipates) complex human issues. Simple questions are designed to help you unlock complicated mind-sets.

Aimed

Your questions must be well thought out and able to pierce through the tiny cracks in your customers' mental armor in a simple, disarming way, much like a beam of sunshine finds it's way through a hole in the fence. To aim means to be precise, targeted, focused, and purposeful.

Jesus was a master at this. He asked Peter, "Have you any food?" then He went on to prove His identity by having Peter cast his nets on the other side of the boat, only to make the largest catch of fish ever. Then, as they were eating, Jesus asked several more questions that revealed Peter's heart and effectively reinstated him. Peter went on to fulfill his destiny. Jesus' approach was to ask salty questions that caused the hearers to discover motives and needs they didn't realize they had. Such questions prepare prospects to receive what you have to say.

Leading

You should know where you are trying to lead someone with your questions. Your goal is to lead customers or listeners to an understanding of their needs, then how your solution meets that need. All too often salespeople try to present their solution without understanding their customers' real needs.

I joined a client once as he called on one of his customers. It turned out that the customer had just ordered a piece of equipment from one of the cheaper competitors. I asked the customer a series of leading questions, which caused him to understand that he had completely overlooked the most important requirement of dependability. When we walked out of his office, we had an order for my client's piece of equipment, which was priced 25% higher but delivered the dependability that was most needed. We got that sale with leading questions, not with product knowledge or a slick presentation. When you ask leading questions, the customer provides the answers you're both looking for!

Questions unlock motivation, motivation reveals need, understanding need is the basis for acquisition, and acquisition and selling are necessary to succeed in the world of sales. Sales are made based on what customers say, not on what you say. If you're trying to convince people to purchase your product, you will have far more success if you discover their point of need. That is best done through questions.

Timely

Your questions are especially relevant at the time you ask them. I asked a businessman several pinpoint questions to see if he was ready to submit his life to Christ, to which he replied, "If you had asked me that question ten years ago, I would have declined, but right at this moment, I am ready." No matter what you are offering, timing is everything. Your questions must reveal a need that is meaningful at that precise moment.

Besides being timely, your questions must be relevant, uncover a present need, and reveal something that will motivate the listener to take immediate action.

Making a sale is a result of...

Serving

Asking

Listening

Excelling

I was once asked to do some customized sales training with a company that had been trained for ten years by a firm that taught lying as an acceptable way to secure an appointment. Other sales techniques had been taught, and learned, that basically pitted the salesman against the customer. The result was stagnant sales for several years.

The company's sales force was in desperate need of a new approach. They needed to learn what a SALE really was. A SALE is a combination of Serving, Asking, Listening, and Excelling. Unless you approach the sales profession with an attitude of service to the customer, you will by default approach it with the idea of "using" the customer to meet your income requirements. That is inherently wrong and strategically doomed.

Many people feel guilty for making a sale. This is because they see selling as something they do to someone for their gain rather than something they do with someone for mutual gain. We must begin and end the day with an attitude of service. This attitude must be inside your heart, woven into the fabric of your life view. Look for unselfish ways you can serve both your customers and your potential customers, and see if that doesn't make a difference in the outcome.

Serving

The Serving part is extremely important and must be an attitude of the heart. If you serve someone merely out of a hope of a reward, you may receive some reward, but nothing approaching the rewards of a heart posture of service. When you have a genuine joy to see other people have their desires met, two things happen. First, they are far better served because you will always go the extra mile, and second, you get a feeling of inner satisfaction by knowing that you helped them in a special and meaningful way.

In the process of serving in the business community, you can be well rewarded for your effort. I believe that serving must be at the heart of your motivation. Customers can often pick up on your motivation, if not consciously, then subconsciously. Oftentimes, they buy in spite of your motivation, not because of it.

Asking

If you have settled your motivational issues and are truly seeking to serve customers, you must learn what their needs truly are. That begins with well thought out, deliberate questions with a purpose.

A group of experienced sales reps I trained were told to develop a quality questioning strategy and then to ask questions with a servant's motivation. Instead of trying to be more persuasive or slick, they were to listen to their customers needs. The results were a 21% increase in sales the first month, a 55% increase the second month, and an average of about 45% over the first six months.

Listening

Before you can ask good questions, you first need be a good listener. A lot of salesmen fail to hear what the customers are saying. The customers' cry is "to be understood," and only after they are understood are they ready to understand you.

When the blind man approached Jesus to be healed, Jesus didn't say, "I know what you need. Here, receive your sight." Instead, Jesus asked the man what he wanted. He took time to listen. He took time to ask, even though He knew why the man was there. After He had asked, He demonstrated that He was listening by thoroughly meeting the blind man's need.

If you want to excel in sales, it's not enough to ask good questions, you must listen intently with the purpose of answering those questions in a way that will thoroughly satisfy the one asking them. If you're going to the trouble of asking good questions, the least you can do is listen carefully. Here are a few tips to help you listen more effectively:

Twelve Keys to Compassionate Listening

1. Maintain eye contact - Looking at the prospect compels you to listen.

2. Notify your body - Smile, nod or communicate with body language that you are listening.

3. Give verbal feedback - It affirms the prospect.

4. Be relaxed - It relaxes the prospect.

5. Read between the lines - Look for the real message.

6. Give them the floor - Don't outdo the prospect with your stories.

7. Be aware of "personal space" - Be careful of "touchy feely" behavior.

8. Be sincere - Authenticity carries the day!

9. Ask questions - Shows you're listening.

10. Take notes - Shows that you value what is being said and that you are taking it seriously.

11. Ignore distractions – Remain focused on the customer.

12. Be interested - Make that choice!

Excelling

Excelling is all about delivering your promise in such a way as to fully meet—if not exceed—the customers' expectations. Talk is cheap, because promises made do not always equal promises kept in today's business arena.

The saying, "Promise small and deliver big," is true in principle, but in today's business environment, small promises don't usually gain much attention. We must promise substantively and still deliver. Go the extra mile with your customers. Deliver on smaller promises along the way, like returning their calls promptly, being on time for appointments, and giving personal attention to customer service. When you excel in the small things, they will believe you for the bigger things.

12

How to Uncover Your Customers' Pain

Before planning the Canaanite conquest, Moses wanted answers to seven questions. He sent twelve spies into the land on a reconnaissance mission to gather that information. The information would later be used to stage a brilliant military campaign. There are several parallels between Moses' military conquest and our conquest of a sales territory or a key account.

Like the Promised Land, sales offer tremendous opportunity and substantial opposition. Planning, skill, precision and strategy are needed to succeed. Why not adapt a biblical role model like Moses, who brought modern civilization the foundational laws of civil government, since others have adapted the leadership style of Attila the Hun to their business dealings?

The seven questions Moses asked are found in Numbers 13:17-20. When I first saw these, I took a few days to ponder the implications of each question, then tried to make it applicable to the sales process. It sounded good, but I wanted to see if it really worked in the rough and tumble world of sales.

At that time a new client of mine, the president of an air-conditioner equipment wholesale company, told me about a contractor that he and his sales manager had been calling on twice a month for six years to have him carry their brand of air conditioning equipment. They had bought him and his crew breakfast, lunch and dinner (the good ol' boy way of selling), gone to movies together, and even shared a meal in each other's homes, but had never done any real business together.

The bi-monthly call was about to take place, and the president asked me for advice. I told him there were seven questions he ought to ask the contractor. He thought that sounded a little strange, so I explained that they weren't really seven questions as much as they were seven topics, and under each topic I wrote out a handful of questions that he could choose from to ask.

He called on the contractor armed with these new questions, and being unfamiliar with their content, simply read from the prepared sheet and recorded the contractor's responses. In the process of asking those questions, he uncovered areas of need and interest that had gone undetected for the previous six years. As a result, he was able to make a proposal based on his new findings and within forty-eight hours of the initial call, he had obtained a purchase order for $60,000!

He wondered whether it was the questioning strategy or just lucky timing, so he called a meeting of his sales force and told them that he wasn't sure what my questioning strategy was or why it worked, but he wanted everyone using it from then on. It was the end of March and they were about to begin their April selling cycle and decided to compare their April results with the previous April where they had generated about $1.2 million in sales revenue. They were hoping for about $1.3 million, but were amazed to find that they actually wrote over $1.7 million in sales!

When I told the president where the questions came from, he was very surprised, but the results spoke for themselves.

The Moses strategy for questioning

"Then Moses sent them to spy out the land of Canaan, and said to them, 'Go up this way into the South, and go up to the mountains, and see the land, (1) What it is? (2) Whether the people who dwell in it are strong or weak? (3) Few or many? (4) Whether the land they dwell in is good or bad? (5) Whether the cities they inhabit are tents or strongholds? (6) Whether the land is fat or lean? (7) And whether there is any wood? Be of good

courage and bring some of the fruit of the land'"
(Numbers 13:17-20).

1 — Circumstantial questions & lay of the land: *What it is?* "

It's true that people "don't care how much you know until they know how much you care." The purpose of circumstantial questioning is to learn more about your customers' work. They pour a great deal of their lives into working for a company and usually appreciate it when someone takes an interest in what they do.

The second reason for this line of questioning is to find out what the company values or takes pride in, such as "on-time" delivery, excellent service, or professionalism. This is important information to know when it comes time to discuss the benefits of what you have to offer so you can tie in your strong points to the ones they consider very important in their own business. It's hard for customers who say they have great quality products to minimize the importance of your quality.

The third reason for circumstantial questioning is it puts customers at ease. When you ask non-threatening, easy to answer questions, you begin to "break the ice" and develop rapport. The following questions are good icebreakers and demonstrate a genuine interest in the prospects and what they are all about, and they serve to help you identify multiple decision-makers in the buying process:

- What is the nature of your business?
- How long have you been in business?
- How many locations do you have?
- How many employees do you have?
- How does your business compare in size to competitors?
- What share of the market do you have in your area?
- What is the state of the industry?
- Who are your main competitors?
- What are your competitors' strong points?
- What separates you from your competition?
- What are your strengths in the marketplace?
- What are some of the challenges you are facing?
- What have you been most successful at?

2— The competition: *"Whether the people who dwell in it are strong or weak?"*

Don't be afraid to let prospects identify the strengths of your competitor. It's better to know what you are up against and what the prospects expect you to do. Furthermore, you may be able to better meet their needs in a different way. Avoid taking an offensive posture against the competition. It's okay if the prospect does, but you shouldn't. Listen for strengths you can match or exceed and weak areas you can really assist in.

Several questions you can ask to learn more about your competition are:

- Who are you currently using to supply your needs?

- Who is your sales rep? (This indicates the level of relationship they have)

- What is it about your current supplier you like most?

- What would a perfect relationship with a supplier look like to you?

- How would that perfect relationship help your business?

- If you were a 51% owner of your current supplier and you could change anything about the way they do business with you, what would that be?

- If you were a majority owner in our business and were advising me as to what I could do to interest this company in the services we offer, what advice would you give me?

3— Nail down the scope of your competitions' strengths & weaknesses: *"Few or many?"*

This is where you find out why your prospects like or dislike their current supplier or method of doing business, along with some understanding of what it's costing them to not make a change.

Here are several questions that will help:

- You mentioned you really liked the way your current supplier does such and such, why is that important to you? How does it help your business or help you to do your job better?

- You mentioned that you have experienced some frustration with your current supplier. How did that affect your business? Can you give me an example of when that happened? How did that make you feel?

- If you were to estimate what that might have cost you, what would that number be? How frequently does that happen? So would you say that on an annual basis it's costing you X amount?

4— The opportunity: *"Is the land good or bad?"*

In sales, what you want to uncover quickly is whether or not your call represents a "good" and meaningful opportunity for the prospect, yourself and your company.

In every business there are a few questions you can ask that will quickly determine whether there is a basis to continue. If a man just purchased a brand new car last month, he is not likely to be in the market for another one. If he just refinanced his home, he's probably not in the market for a new mortgage.

The word translated "bad" means distressful, calamitous, adverse or wrong. There are some customers who may look good on the surface but doing business with them could be calamitous. Therefore, this question includes the idea of qualifying the prospects in a financial sense. Do they have the means to exercise a purchase should they want to? Are you dealing with someone who has the authority to either approve or secure that approval? If you're attempting to sell a ten thousand-dollar piece of equipment to someone who doesn't have the authority to buy toilet paper, you're probably wasting your time. Are they the kind of customer you want? Maybe you're the tenth supplier they've gone through in the last 12 months. Maybe they don't pay their bills.

I've heard of several companies that have done business with very large corporate behemoths and after investing considerable resources to win the sale and supply the goods, found themselves waiting for three to six months to get paid, straining their cash flow and crippling their business. Some of the following questions will help you discover the answers:

- Have you made a recent purchase of this kind of product?
- How often do you purchase this kind of product normally?
- When it comes to making decisions regarding which supplier you use, who has that final responsibility and are there others involved in the decision?
- How long have you had your current supplier?
- Who was your previous supplier? Why did you change?
- Do you have much employee turnover?
- If we were given the opportunity to be your supplier, what would you expect from us in terms of service, quality, credit terms, etc.?

- Do you have money in the budget for this kind of acquisition?

- When it comes to approving this kind of expenditure, is there anyone else who has to approve this?"

5— Is the prospect or competition thinking short-term or long-term?
"Whether the cities they inhabit are tents or strongholds?"

What kind of vision do your prospects have for their business? Are they using short-term thinking (tents) to solve their problem? Is the competition making short-term recommendations that are merely a quick fix but not a long-term (stronghold) solution? If so, they are vulnerable to a credible supplier who will offer strong, secure, long-term solutions. See whether the competition is taking advantage of your prospects through pricing, poor service, etc. Your sales strategy will vary depending on whether your competitor has built a stronghold of excellent customer service, fair pricing and good quality or a city of tents, something not capable of withstanding the first credible challenge that comes along.

One of my clients sold industrial cutting equipment such as lathes for use in manufacturing metal goods. I was asked to spend a day with one of their sales reps to discover why such a bright, pleasant fellow was failing so miserably at sales. As we were on our way to the first call, I asked him what the purpose of this call was. He explained that the owner had requested a brochure and quote on some equipment a couple of months back and he wanted to stop by and see if he was still interested. Besides the fact that he had allowed two months to elapse on someone who had already demonstrated interest, he was quite unprepared to take whatever we might have found to the next level.

The owner greeted us at the door with, "You're too late. I've already purchased from one of your competitors." The salesman was surprised and embarrassed and started politely to back out when I asked the owner if he had already received delivery of the equipment and if he had signed an agreement and made payment? He indicated in the affirmative on all three accounts.

"Before leaving," I said, "I'm helping this company improve their customer service and I would love to see your new piece of equipment in operation to get an idea of what you were looking for." He gladly took me back to the plant where the machine was in full production and proudly proclaimed that he had purchased it for $53,000 instead of the $68,000 my client wanted for his unit.

I knew nothing about the equipment and couldn't have even found the on/off switch, let alone explain how it worked. But I didn't have to understand the equipment until I first understood the customer, so I proceeded with questions.

"How long has it been installed?" I asked.

"About a month now," he replied. "We had it for a thirty day trial and just purchased it yesterday."

"How's it been working for you?"

"Great," he exclaimed.

After hearing the machine make a peculiar clunking noise, I asked, "What was that noise?"

He replied, "I don't know."

"What do you make with this machine?"

"Precision parts," he said simply.

"When the machine makes that noise, does that affect the precision of the part being made?"

"Yes. This actually happened during the trial but they came out and supposedly fixed it." This was interesting, so I said, "Really. How long did it take to get service?"

"Well," he replied, "that was a bit frustrating. It took them three days to respond."

Things were getting warm now. "Really? And this was when they were trying their best to win you over as a customer?"

He nodded, "Yes."

"What level of service do you think they will provide you now that they have your money?"

"Actually," he said, "they've just got a down payment."

I asked, "Tell me, what did you do for three days when the machine was shut down?"

Even he was getting warm now. "It caused quite a bottleneck in our assembly line."

Playing ignorant, I said, "What happens when that happens?"

"Our orders get backed up, we have late deliveries and we might have to lay off some workers," he explained.

"Sounds expensive," I replied. "How much did you mention that you saved on this purchase?"

"About $15,000."

"Hmmm," I said, "you mentioned that you make precision parts with this machine. When the machine clunks, what happens to the part being made at the time?"

He creased his brow and said, "It's supposed to go in the scrap pile, but many times it ends up in a customer's order."

"What happens when the customer gets a faulty part?"

"They're not very happy about it," he said honestly.

"Could it cost you a customer?" I probed.

"Yes, it could."

"What might that be worth?"

"Plenty," he sighed.

As I was asking how frequently that occurred, the machine operator walked by and said, with evident frustration, that as a company they have seventy-two hours to cancel their order from the time of signing the agreement.

I turned to the owner and asked what I already knew, "When did you sign the agreement?"

"Yesterday," he stated.

"So," I said calmly, "What would you like to do now?" He quickly replied, "Let's go to lunch and discuss it."

Over lunch it became clear that the extra $15,000 for a better piece of equipment would save him far more over the next few years. When we got back to the office, he exercised his right of cancellation, issued my client a purchase order and gave him a down payment on the spot!

Most sales people would have done what that rep was about to do—walk out the door without asking any questions—and tell their boss that they bought the competitive unit because it was $15,000 cheaper. Needless to say, there were a lot of mistakes being made by that sales rep and it was well worth their investment to discover them, but that rep went on to succeed with the company after making his first sale that day. The point is that the sale was made mostly through questioning.

The questions you ask and the answers your customers give are far more important than any presentation material you may have. Remember that the sale is made based on what the customers say, not on what you say. Therefore, never tell customers something you can ask them.

6— Their system: *"Is the land fat or lean?"*

The word "fat" means "plenteous" and the word "lean" means "thin or famished." In sales, what we want to find out is whether the system of doing things has been fruitful or productive for your prospects. Is their current system yielding a good financial return for them? Compared to what? Is it "famished," costing them a small fortune and they don't know it?

I once called on a lumber mill that had an old copier making 2,000 copies per month at ten cents per copy on special thermal paper. New copiers operated at two and a half cents per copy and used regular plain paper. The saving was evident. Their current system was lean, famished, and was costing them money. They thought because they owned it outright that they were ahead of the game, but they weren't.

Your goal is to learn what the competition and/or the clients have accomplished under their current way of doing things. What you're really looking for is whether or not the way they are doing things has been productive or costly. If so, how productive or how costly? If productive, you want to find out whether they are at maximum potential. Oftentimes, customers are happy with the results they are achieving simply because they have never had anything to compare it with.

It helps to ask these questions:

- Is what you're doing now working the way you had hoped?

- Have you compared those results to what is available now?

- Do you know if a better result is possible?

- Are you getting the results you planned on?

- If you keep on doing what you've always been doing, you'll keep on getting what you've always been getting. Insanity is doing the same thing over and over and expecting a different result. What result were you hoping for?

- Do you think there is room for improvement?

- Why do you feel you haven't realized that result yet?

- Do you have any idea what your current way of doing things is costing you in terms of reduced production? Lost opportunity? Higher scrap rates? Missed business? Cash flow management?

· What plans do you have to change that?

· What kind of timeframe are you working on?

· Who is else shares the responsibility for the decision that got you where you are today?"

7— Their goals: *"Is there any wood?"*

Wood fuels a fire and without it, nothing happens. In the same way, goals fuel a company or person's growth. Your goal is to find a way to come alongside your customers to help them meet their goals with your product or service. Though it is often neglected, this is an extremely important area to explore. They may have production goals, sales goals, quality goals, or some combination of those to meet an internal company goal. Perhaps their goal is more subjective, like getting a promotion, raise, or bonus. Regardless of what their goals are, listen and see how what you have to offer will help them reach their goals. When customers see you as someone working with them to achieve a common goal, instead of someone sparring with them to meet your own goals, you will have a much better chance of succeeding.

I was with a sales rep calling on an existing customer when I suggested we ask questions about goals and vision. The sales rep was nice enough, but felt questions about goals and vision were irrelevant, so I ended up asking the questions. As the purchasing agent and I talked, the answers led to more questions, which yielded more information than had previously been known to the sales rep. About thirty minutes into the interview, the sales rep interrupted our conversation and apologized to the customer for never asking the kind of questions I was asking. He simply had no idea of the wealth of information that was there to uncover and how he could use that information to better serve the customer. The sales rep and his company went on to improve and increase the level of service they provided to many of their bigger accounts.

Several good questions to ask about goals and vision are:

- What are your goals for the year?
- Do you have production goals? Sales goals? Quality goals? How are you doing on those goals?
- What do you think needs to be done differently? What are you doing about that?
- What is the mission for the company? Are you fulfilling that mission?
- Where do you want to be five years from now in this business?
- What are your long-term objectives for the company? What is your plan to achieve these goals? How's it going? What will be the reward if you reach your objectives?
- In your opinion, what's the most important way a company like ours can help a company like yours reach its goals?

According to one survey, a person asking five or more questions closed seventy-two percent more business than a person asking only two questions. But asking questions is only part of the answer. You need to ask the right questions if you're going to get your prospects to open up and give you the information you need to serve them best and make a sale.

8— Make an advance! *"Bring back some of the fruit of the land!"*

In addition to the seven questions Moses wanted answers for, he instructed his men to bring back some of the fruit of the land. He was saying, "Don't come back empty-handed."

In sales, this means that we should never leave an appointment without some form of commitment for a next step, which should always be specific and include a time frame. Sales reps often leave a call with something like, "Well, let me know what you think." This leaves the call very open ended with no agreement for action. Doing this assures you that at best you will start your next contact with this customer at the same place you left it. At worst, you will find that the customer purchased from a competitor who was willing to make an advance and even close the sale. Always leave with something in hand, whether it be a purchase order, a down payment or simply an agreed upon follow-up appointment. This gives purpose and expectation to your next call while building a firewall between your prospect and the competition.

Uncovering the Pain

On top of the questioning strategy it is possible to lay a simple model that will help you bring your questions to a focal point and uncover the pain that your customers have and which you can help relieve. It's called a PAIN index...

Problem (Ask the customers where it hurts.)

Assess (Ask them the cause & effect of that problem.)

Implications (What happens when this happens?)

Next? (What would you like to see happen?)

During the course of your questioning if you uncover an area of pain or concern, ask for the cause of that pain and the effect of that problem. Always take the effect to the next step by asking the implications of that problem, and if possible, get the customers to tell you a story about when that painful episode occurred. Then ask them what they would like to see happen next. Get an idea of what they see as a solution while simultaneously leaving the responsibility on their shoulders to solve it. Once you've got those answers, you're ready to move on. Here is an example:

Problem

Seller: "If you could change anything about your current system, what would you change?"

Buyer: "I would change the way it processes documents." (Prospect just inferred pain.)

Seller: "What happens now?"

Buyer: "It's just entirely too slow."

Seller: "What do you mean by too slow?"

Buyer: "Well, it takes a week to get a document through our system and it should only take one day." (Prospect just admitted pain.)

Assess: (Cause of the pain)

Seller: "What do you think is the cause of the delay?"

Buyer: "There are too many people handling the paperwork."

Assess: (Effect of the pain)

Seller: "What is the effect of that delay on your business process?"

Buyer: "Well, it slows down our invoicing and affects our cash flow."

Implications

Seller: "What happens when that happens?"

Buyer: "I get a lot of heat from the president of the company."

Seller: "Can you give me an example of a situation where that happened?"

Buyer: "About three months ago, we were paying a lot of big bills while really lagging behind on our invoicing and ..."

Next?

Seller: "What would you like to see happen to correct this?"

Use this PAIN index all through the questioning process. Whenever you uncover pain, always find the cause and effect, along with the implications and their ideas of what to do next.

Once you have walked through all of the buyers' pain, ask them by what criteria they will be evaluating potential vendors. This simple but often overlooked question can make all the difference in winning the sale. You may think they will be evaluating based on price or perhaps quality, but maybe their priority this time is meeting a particular delivery schedule, so always ask the criteria by which you and other vendors will be evaluated. Then, when you present your solution, you can keep selling to their highest need and the criteria they spelled out as being most important.

13

How to Handle Objections

People tend to surface objections only when they are seriously considering the offer. Objections aren't a bad thing; they are the customer's way of saying, "Help me over my hurdles so I can purchase your product."

Once when I was training a co-worker who was struggling to make it in sales, we made a callback on a prospect who had been evaluating our equipment on a trial basis. The prospect informed us upon our arrival that he had made the decision to keep his old equipment and thanked us for allowing him to try out the new equipment. The struggling salesman immediately started preparing the trial copier for shipment back to the office.

I asked the owner how he arrived at that decision, and he explained it was just a matter of finances. He didn't have an extra five thousand dollars to spend right then, so I asked him if he had considered the lease option, which he said he had but still would need about seven hundred dollars to initiate the lease. I asked him if he would consider letting us use his old copier as a trade-in and apply the trade allowance against his first few lease payments. We could even delay his first real cash payment until nearly the end of the year. Well, that settled it for him. He said he would take it and signed the lease agreement.

When he left the room to go get his checkbook, the sales rep I was with said, "No wonder I'm not doing very well; I can't be pushy like you." His comment frustrated me, because I've made it a point in selling not to be pushy. When the owner returned, I told him the concern of the other sales rep and asked him if he felt in any way pressured and if so to please let me know and we would tear up the contract. He told me that he hadn't felt the slightest bit pressured, but that he simply had some concerns and he was glad that I was able to help him through them. That's what handling objections is all about.

Objections come in two basic shapes. They are either invalid, requiring clearing up a misunderstanding, or they are valid and require an answer to put it in perspective

Valid Objections

Here are some simple guidelines to consider using with valid objections:

1.   Clarify by restating the objection as a question.
2.   Empathize with the prospect.
3.   Minimize by putting the concern in perspective.
4.   Validate. Offer evidence. Provide a compelling reason for your position.

Here is an example:

Clarify
"So if I understand you correctly, you're concerned about the amount of the initial investment. Is that correct?"

Empathize
"I can certainly understand why price would be very important to you. My hope is that you will select the 'partner' who will give you the greatest value."

Minimize (put it in perspective)
"When you spread the price difference over the life of the work being done, we're talking about pennies-a-day difference. What many of my customers have found is that 'price' is only part of the overall equation for comparing competing solutions. What they're most interested in evaluating is Return On Investment and the risk/reward calculations."

Validate

"A solid company with an excellent track record of proven performance and industry leadership will seldom be the lowest bidder. But if you evaluate your decision on the basis of Return On Investment, you will find the quality of our work will ensure the best overall return."

Invalid Objections

1. Clarify by restating objection as a question
2. Empathize with the prospect.
3. Deny and correct.
4. Validate.

Here is an example:

Clarify

"So if I understand you correctly, your concern about doing business with us is our inability to process metric claims and that's very important to you. Is that correct?"

Empathize

"I can certainly understand why you would feel it was important to have one vendor processing all your claims."

Deny and Correct

"But apparently there's been some misunderstanding because not only do we process metric claims, but our customers tell us it's the most thorough and cost effective metric processing work they've ever had done."

Validate

"In fact, we just completed a huge project for Company X in another state. I'd be delighted for you to call them."

Another approach with invalid objections is the Feel, Felt, and Found approach. You say things like, "I understand how you feel about.... We have had other customers who have felt the same way.... But they have found that...."

Handling Objections

The main thing to remember in handling objections is to treat customers with dignity. Answer the objection straight on and make sure they are satisfied with your answer. Here are seven common reasons why customers offer resistance:

1. Lack of Need:

Sometimes salespeople try to sell something that the prospect has no need or want for. Your job is not to create need, but rather to uncover need.

2. Lack of Trust:

The prospect hasn't found a basis to trust you, your product or your company. Your job is to find out what the trust issue is and then, using the seven ways to create a climate of trust, melt their resistance and win their loyalty.

3. Lack of Respect:

Sometimes a sales rep will work for a great company, have an excellent product, but personally present a less than professional image. This may take the shape of poor product knowledge, lack of familiarity with the account, or poor communication skills. All of which can be corrected if the rep has the desire.

4. Lack of Relationship:

Sometimes there is a personality clash between the buyer and the sales rep that at least temporarily is irreconcilable. Instead of forcing the personalities together, find someone within your organization who can team up with you and help out in this account. The lady who hated my boss and the copier company I worked for was not mad at me, but I knew she didn't want a salesman calling her, so I had the technician handle the follow-up under my direction. I stayed at a distance until she warmed up, then we resumed the face-to-face selling process, which resulted in an order.

5. Lack of Ability:

Sometimes customers offer resistance because they don't have the authority to say "yes" and don't want to admit it to you. You might have to dig a little deeper through other resources to find out whether this person has any real authority, but as long as you're not asking them, they may keep on snowing you.

6. Lack in the Product:

A client initially turned down a proposal for sales training, claiming that it was too expensive. He wanted to try it with one sales rep. We didn't offer individual training programs, so we solved the problem by increasing what we were offering to do, more than quintupling the price. The company was very satisfied with both the proposal and the result and later came back for another customized program for another division. The total investment was over seven times the original proposition, but the customer got what he wanted and had a terrific return on the investment that year.

Sometimes you have to make what you have match what customers want.

7. Lack of Funds:

It's amazing how people can find funds when they want to. For example, if I was asking you to spend $5,000 for a new entertainment center, you might tell me you couldn't afford that right now. But if I had a box of 10,000 silver dollars in my attic and said you could have them for half price if you'd come haul them off for me, I'll bet you would find the $5,000 in a real hurry (assuming it was a legitimate offer). Sometimes you need to help customers find the funds by creating a legitimate sense of urgency. This may mean that you simply need to sell them a lesser model that fits their budget and then move on to the next opportunity.

When to answer objections
The three best times to answer objections are:

1. Before the concern is raised
If there's an objection that you commonly hear and routinely expect, it's probably best to raise the concern first. For example, if you know that your price is often raised as a concern, then you might consider saying something like, "The investment for our service is higher than a lot of others due to the tremendous value we include with this service. By the time I'm finished the presentation, I'm sure you will agree that it is the best value and provides the highest return for every dollar invested."

2. When the concern is raised
During a presentation you may be interrupted with a concern about some aspect of your product. Generally speaking, if it's an easy concern to answer, do it right then and there. If it represents a major detour in your presentation and you know you're going to be covering that later, explain that you will be covering that in a few minutes and ask if you can defer until then. On the other hand, if it's painfully obvious that the buying authority asking the question won't be paying much attention to you until his question is answered, you may have to answer it when it is asked.

3. Postpone until later

Many times the question being posed will take you off on a side trail and derail or at least slow the momentum of your presentation. If at all possible (unless it's something really simple), postpone your answer until the end of your presentation.

Three tips to avoid price tensions

Your objective when it comes to price negotiations should be to agree on the highest margin and most favorable terms possible, while treating customers with complete fairness and providing value equal to, or greater than, the agreed upon financial settlement. To do this well, you will need to believe in your value proposition, know how to negotiate, operate with integrity and understand your competition.

Tip 1: *There is hardly anything in the world that someone cannot make a little worse and sell a little cheaper.*

There are usually good reasons why your product costs more than a competitor's product, such as the use of brass instead of plastic, leather instead of vinyl, etc. The designer felt that those extra components needed to be in the product and that the cost justified the benefit. Too often, however, the sales team has little or no knowledge as to the real reasons why their product is priced higher than their competition. Make a point to find out the cost justification. What are the benefits to customers? How can those benefits be measured?

How can you provide a cost justification that will make sense to your customers?

Tip 2: *Price is not the only factor.*

Over the years I've heard that nearly one in four people buy on price alone. If you can't convince your customers to buy on value instead of price, you need to move on and leave those low profit deals for your competition to haggle over, while you work on the more lucrative ones yourself. Remember that part of the value they are getting by dealing with you is you! That's one thing your competition doesn't have. Make sure that it's something customers see as a great value. Be a resource to your customers. Make every visit count and always deposit something of value in their memory of dealing with you.

Tip 3: *Price is a relative thing.*

When customers tell you that your price is "a lot of money," you need to find out, "In comparison to what?" Perhaps $100,000 is a lot of money for a software program, but compared to the savings that will occur as a result, it may only be a drop in a bucket. If you are told that your price is expensive compared to the competition, make sure that you are comparing apples with apples. Many times your competition will bid a job differently, thus giving the appearance that they have found a lower price for the same service. Take the time necessary to see if your service is truly more expensive.

What does "too expensive" mean?

$!—"It's over my budget."

Customers may say that your product has great value, but they simply don't have the budget. Either find a way to make it affordable by helping them find the money, or move on to the next prospect.

$!—"It's not worth it."

Here the customers are saying they can afford it, but they simply don't see the value to them. Perhaps they don't have any pain or they don't see it as a good solution for solving their pain. Review their pain issues and how your solution addresses their pain. If they are still skeptical, offer names of satisfied customers for them to call, or better yet, have the prospect call one of your customers on the spot.

$!—"It's more than I need."

If your customers say this, it means that your service or product is a good deal with good value and they can afford it, but it's just more than they can responsibly justify for the need that they have. Your might consider offering a lesser version of the same product.

Price negotiations

A very important consideration to remember as clients move across the continuum towards a sale is that cost justification and price negotiation are two different things. For example, you decide that you want a new car, so you read about various cars you've been admiring. At first you admire the trendy deluxe models, then reality sets in and you decide on a good quality car. Now that you've cost-justified a certain new car, you begin to negotiate price.

Naturally, the buyer wrings the washcloth for every drop, and the seller is the washcloth. (When do you stop wringing a washcloth? When it stops dripping!) The buyer has an emotional need now, which is to know that he's also getting the best deal possible.

The better your cost-justification earlier in the sales process the easier to hold your price later. If you make concessions, give away soft items like service or more product. And be willing to walk away from the deal if necessary.

14
Presentation Strategies & Closings

From a sales rep's perspective, the selling process in its simplest form goes through a five-step process.

Five steps to selling

Step 1 — You see the need

At times, customers see the need first and call you to help them fill that need, but those are more the exception than the rule. More commonly, the seller calls on prospects and engages them in conversation. The prospects hear the seller say something that makes them think they have a need or an interest in the seller's product or service. The seller directs the conversation through a well thought out series of questions. In the process of learning the answers, a need begins to surface and the seller is usually the first to see it.

Step 2— They see the need

Once you have discovered a legitimate need for your product or service, lead the buyer to an awareness of that need through the questioning process we have already discussed.

Step 3— You see the solution

When you have gained an understanding that a general need for your product or service exists, further questioning and analysis of their circumstances will enable you to see the ideal solution.

Step 4— They see the solution

Armed with all the data you uncovered in your questioning sequence and possibly through a needs analysis, present your findings in a clear, concise and compelling manner that causes your customers to see the solution.

Step 5— Close the sale

Paint the picture of what it looks like to put-off this decision compared to the pay-off for taking the appropriate action. Then, ask the buyer what he would like to do next based on both the findings you have uncovered and the solution you have presented.

Once you see the solution, it's time to cause the buyer to see the solution. The process for conveying the solution will vary greatly depending on your product or service, the size of investment, and the authority of the person you are presenting to. Your presentation may simply be a product demonstration followed by cost justification and proof statements. It might include a "Power Point" presentation complete with executive summary, situation analysis, recommendations, investment schedule, implementation schedule, return-on-investment schedule, and a layout of what the next steps look like. Regardless, the principles of presenting a solution remain the same.

Seven principles of presenting a solution

1. Review of Findings
2. Review of Conclusions
3. Pre-Commitment
4. Recommendations
5. Investment
6. Cost Justification
7. Close/Confirm theSale

1. Review of Findings

Begin your presentation by summarizing what you discovered through the interview process, possibly including input from any field analysis, employee surveys, equipment or system evaluation, etc. you have done. Your review might go something like this:

"Bob, you mentioned in our discussion that you were concerned about the age of your present equipment and the potential loss if it were to give out unexpectedly. You also mentioned that you were concerned about the productivity, or lack thereof, even when it's running optimally and you stated you would be open to evaluating more up-

to-date options that included smart chips and laser technology. When we spoke with your current machine operators, they told us they were experiencing some serious quality issues and generating excessive waste materials, particularly when building titanium parts. In fact, they indicated that the waste was a large reason for the recent cost overruns that have been plaguing your production line."

2. Review of Conclusions

Conclusions are simply what the findings mean to the buyer. Take a moment and recap the implications of your findings, including any financial ramifications if possible. For example:

"Bob, when we talked about the threat of your equipment failing unexpectedly, you indicated that it could likely stop the entire production line with an estimated economic impact of at least $100,000. I believe you mentioned that it might have some negative impact on your job if it was found out that it was preventable. On the productivity side, it looks as though you are actually operating at about thirty percent of what's possible with smart-chip and laser technology and I will show you what the increase in productivity looks like in terms of increased savings in just a few minutes. The quality issue seemed to be more far reaching than we had both anticipated. According to the Vice President of Sales, there has been some erosion of your customer base due to unacceptable failure rates of the parts you produce and one of your key accounts is now going out to bid on future orders. The loss of business and the potential loss of key accounts that are known to be at risk represent well over a million dollars in revenue this year alone and dwarf any cost overruns due to excessive wasting of titanium. All in all, it appears we have more than ample reason to pursue better alternatives than your current system and equipment."

3. Pre-Commitment

The teeth in this pre-commitment will vary, depending on whether you are going to be closing for the opportunity to present the entire solution at the next board meeting or asking for the order. Either way, you will be asking for a decision. It could go like this:

"If we can demonstrate to your satisfaction that our new smart-chip, laser lathe can generate real savings by dramatically reducing production time, while simultaneously improving quality and eliminating the threat of imminent break-down and that we can do this cost effectively with an impressive return-on-investment, will we have a basis for doing business?"

4. Recommendations

This is where you demonstrate your ability to meet their needs. This may be done with a live, in-house product demonstration or simply through an oral or visual presentation. The critical elements remain the same. They are...

Fact or feature

Associated Function / Purpose

Validate with Evidence

Obvious Advantage / Benefit

Ratify or Secure Agreement

Fact or Feature: Most products have lots of features. Pick the features that are most relevant to the buyer's highest need and target your presentation to that. Present your features in descending priority. For example, *"Bob, the Super X Lathe has the NASA-developed, high intensity Ram III laser..."*

Associated Function / Purpose: It's not enough to mention a feature. You need to explain its purpose or function relative to their need. With Bob, I would say, *"The Ram III laser will cut through titanium like a hot knife through butter, but without any of the mess..."*

Validate with Evidence: In this case, the best evidence would be an actual demonstration of the laser cutting through titanium, but a video clip, power point presentation or other graphics could suffice. Perhaps you could bring along a titanium part made on the Super X Lathe with the Ram III laser and say, *"Here, let me show you..."*

Obvious Advantage / Benefit: The benefit to your buyers may be clear to you, but make sure you stress the benefit in terms of their need. One of the top Xerox copier salesmen was Gerry Price, who said, "Never state a feature without following through on the benefit by saying, *'And what this means to you is...'"*

For Bob, he would need to hear, *"And what this means to you is your 'cutting time' on titanium parts will be cut by nearly two-thirds, which will speed up production tremendously and eliminate those bottlenecks that have been causing you so much trouble. Being able to produce 'on-time' orders consistently will have a positive impact on your cash flow and customer satisfaction ratings."* Whenever possible, illustrate your point with a relevant third-party story or analogy.

Ratify or Secure Agreement: Before you go on to the next feature of your product or service, you want to make sure the buyer understands your point, and more importantly, agrees with your conclusion. You need to secure agreement by saying something like, *"Can you see how the Ram III will save you significant time on your production line?"* When the buyer gives you his agreement, you should continue with your presentation.

5) Investment

The investment should be clear, easy to understand, and include a choice of terms. Many times I have found that the company who was willing to offer the most creative terms got the business. Sales reps often get nervous about stating the amount of the investment, but that's usually a result of not doing sufficient value justification during the sales process.

6) Value Justification

Any time customers lay out money for a product or service, they want to know what they will receive in return. Ultimately they want to know if the capital outlay justifies the benefits you promise. Anytime you can offer tangible value justification in terms of return-on-investment, you strengthen your case and increase your chances of making the sale, especially if the person you are presenting to has to take those numbers to the boss.

Typically, the investment for your product will be compared to the current cost of doing things, to one of your competitors, or both. When comparing to a less expensive competitor, always remember that you only have to justify the difference in price. For example, if your equipment is $21,500 and your competitor is coming in at $19,900, all you have to do is justify the $1,600 difference in investment, not the entire $21,500. What is the customer going to get from your company for the extra $1,600?

That should be easy for you to answer, especially because they will also be getting your personal support, which no one else can offer. Put the price difference in perspective. If they expect to keep their purchase for at least ten years, then you're only looking at a difference of $160 per year or just under two cents a day difference! That's a small amount to invest for the difference that you bring to the table.

Cost justification against their current system may include time efficiency studies, waste analysis, the impact of improved cash flow, higher customer retention rates, increased sales, reduced deterioration on ancillary equipment, freeing up of other resources, and more. When comparing to their current system or way of doing things, make sure you also factor in the risk of not doing anything, such as the cost of a breakdown and the impact on all the other business processes.

7) Close / Confirm the sale

Throughout the selling process, buyers may exhibit one or more buying signals that indicate they are sold on your proposal. They may ask for a trial period, question you about your terms, start asking you for concessions, inquire about delivery schedules, etc. To find out if they are ready to buy, you can always float a trial balloon. If the customer catches the balloon, he may be ready to buy, but if he sticks a pin in it, you will need to continue selling.

The following acronym from the veteran sales trainer, Carl Stevens, will help you remember the various trial closes you can use:

T— **try a question on a small point** "If you were to decide to get the Super X Lathe, when would you likely want delivery?"

R— **right proposal** "If you were to select our firm as your vendor to replace your old lathes, would you be getting a new stock unit or a custom-designed unit?"

I — **instruction** "If we end up being your vendor for the new lathe equipment, who would we need to schedule for training on its custom features?"

A— **alternate choice** "If you determine that we are the right choice for you, would you want to begin the installation next month or wait until your scheduled shut down?"

L— **let the customer express his feelings** "If you had a vendor you could count on, how would that impact things here?"

C— **challenge** "If you don't find our Super X Lathe to be the best you've seen, there will be no charge for the delivery and pick-up."

L— **littlest** "If we could minimize your overall investment by scheduling all the installations during yur shutdown...?"

O— **offer jump on competition** "If we were able to include X, would that be a meaningful difference to you?"

S— **subtle question** "Have you determined which lathes you want to upgrade first?"

E— **encouragement** "This is the kind of quality work you're looking for, isn't it?"

In today's marketplace, it's no longer a matter of just closing sales, it's a matter of opening relationships. Selling is a mutual journey that you take with your prospects to uncover needs, find solutions, and implement them together. Closing a sale is a beginning, not an end. Asking for the order is much like a marriage proposition. If you were concerned about the answer, you wouldn't ask.

The heart of the sale is in the discovery process as you and the customer, through the questioning process, determine the pain the customer is feeling, along with the cause, effect and implications of that pain. The sale is made based upon what the customer says, not on what you say. Your presentation is merely a feedback that lets him know you understand his pain along with common sense recommendations based on the years of experience you and your company have in relieving his kind of pain.

Making sales

They say a picture is worth a thousand words, but well-known journalist, Eric Severied, once said, "A well-chosen word is worth ten thousand pictures." When you have completed your presentation, having made your case, and you want to secure the commitment to proceed, the following sequence will help you organize your thoughts and make it easier for your customer to say "yes."

This effective approach has helped thousands of people to reach a positive decision. As a business tool, it is effective because it makes sales.

Summarize the needs and implications.

Apply your strengths to their needs & get agreement.

Look ahead to a specific time.

Envision the results of a put-off or pay-off.

Secure commitment.

Sample Closing Arguments

Step 1 Summarize needs & implications:

"John, I understand your primary concern is keeping the plant running. You know that reliable equipment and professional service are essential to reduce your risk of downtime and you'd like to work with a professional vendor who will deliver high-speed efficiency and prompt, reliable service to reduce your risk of missed production goals and the loss of some profit sharing, right?"

Step 2 Apply strengths / Get agreement:

"We've agreed that our smart-chip process will eliminate 98% of the errors you're currently experiencing, correct? I believe we've shown that our Ram III laser will cut down production time by two-thirds, eliminating bottlenecks and increasing customer retention, correct? We've also agreed that our experienced staff and professional service procedures are what you're looking for, right?

Step 3 Look ahead to a specific time:

"John, let's look ahead a year."

Step 4 Envision put-off or pay-off and speak to the Primary Buying Motive:

"Suppose nothing changes and you keep your current system in place for another year. You still have your bottlenecks in the plant, missed delivery dates and a growing number of customer service issues. Or, it's quite possible that during that year, the potential failure that we've been talking about actually happens. Only it happens during a rush production run for one of your key customers and you miss your delivery date and the customer takes all their business to your competitor. Either way John, you lose.

Now compare that with this option. Suppose you choose to invest in the future of your company with the new Super X Lathe. We install the new equipment with smart-chip technology and train all your operators on the new system. During the year, we provide prompt, professional service utilizing the latest in laser correction technology and lathe life extension science. Our patented high tech "smart-chip" laser process and unsurpassed preventive maintenance work together to prevent a failure and subsequent production loss. Either way, you win, and when your production goals are met, your profit sharing goes up!"

Step 5 Secure Commitment:

"Now that's what you really want, isn't it? What do you see as the next step, John?" or *"Where do we go from here?"*

If you have done your questioning well, listened to learn and offered the solution in terms that speak to his pain, closing the sale will simply be a confirmation of what has already happened in his heart through the whole of the process. Closing the sale is simply outlining the terms and conditions of the agreement so the service can proceed and the client can begin experiencing the value statements you've been making.

15

The Secrets to Negotiating

It has been said that in life you don't get what you deserve, you get what you negotiate! Life seems to be an endless series of negotiations with buyers, sellers, merchants, neighbors, siblings, and even our spouses. Is there a reliable Biblical model to apply to our everyday lives? If so, can we categorize it, communicate it and effectively practice it - not to the detriment of any one party - but to the edification and enrichment of all?

Such a model does exist in the New Testament book of Philemon and is outlined by the words of the Apostle Paul. At that time, the world was dominated by Romans and 60% of the population were slaves. It was in this setting that

Paul met Onesimus, who was in all likelihood a runaway slave. Paul led him to Christ and wanted to restore Onesimus to his former slave owner, Philemon.

This was not a simple thing, for under Roman law anyone giving refuge to slaves could be required to pay the owner for the loss of use of the slaves during their absence. Furthermore, runaway slaves could be punished by death if caught! Paul had given refuge to Onesimus, whose name means "profitable," and the purpose in his letter was to persuade Philemon to receive Onesimus back into his home, not as a runaway slave, but as a beloved brother. From church history it is evident that Philemon listened, for Onesimus was restored and eventually went on to become a bishop in the early church.

The art of negotiation

Negotiation is the ability to communicate information that creates a climate of goodwill and favor (instead of fear) in the changing of opinions, circumstances and agreements.

In the sales process, negotiating is much more effective if done after the buyer has made a heart decision to purchase from you. If you begin to negotiate terms, price, delivery, etc., before the buyer has made that decision, you will find yourself in a weaker bargaining position. You only have a limited number of "chips" you can bargain with. Why give them all away before the buyer has settled on the rightness of your product or service offering? Certainly, some concessions up-front can make the buyer more interested in your offer, but it also creates an expectation of more concessions from you with little reciprocal effort.

As you negotiate, it is not necessary to misrepresent anything to have a positive outcome. This type of misrepresentation lays the groundwork for mistrust and without trust an agreement is less likely to be reached. The strategies of negotiation below are not always to be used in every circumstance, but they are excellent models based on the writings of the Apostle Paul for integrity-oriented negotiating and have a proven track record of being highly effective.

Thirty-one successful strategies for win/win negotiations

1. Appeal to the heart (emotions): *"Paul, a prisoner of Christ Jesus..." (vs. 1)*

Paul begins his appeal by reminding Philemon that he is in prison for the gospel. He speaks directly to the heart of his friend. Most experts agree that 90% of any decision is made in the heart and the remaining 10% of the decision is made in the mind where the negotiating takes place. People buy for their reasons, not yours. They buy into a "position" based on emotion and then justify it with logic. When negotiating with people, find a way to appeal to their emotional side. Give them a compelling reason to buy into your "position."

2. Reduce conflict by stressing common goals: *"fellow laborer... fellow soldier" (vs. 1-2)* Focus on things in common versus things that divide. What are the common goals you share with the

other party? If you have a customer who is having difficulties with your product line, neither of you wants that to continue, so your common ground is the desire to find a resolution. Work on the problem from the same side of the fence. Emphasizing common goals reduces conflict and creates an environment for doing business. Get on a common footing with your customers and build on that.

3. Include others to increase the impact of the decision: *"and Timothy our brother... to the beloved Apphia, Archippus... and to the church in your house" (vs. 1-2)*

Identify all who will be impacted by the decision being made, and remind the person you are dealing with of everyone who will be impacted. For example, if you are talking with one of the managers at an industrial plant, you might remind him that the VP of Operations and the VP of Sales have an interest in the outcome. When you remind your prospects of the fact that others will be watching their decisions, it can have a significant impact on the choices they make. Where appropriate, include the others in the decision process. Often a single decision-maker may favor an outcome that serves his personal interest but not that of the company. If you can include others in the process, it makes it very difficult for one person to accomplish a personal, hidden agenda.

4. Express value for the relationship: *"beloved friend... Grace to you and peace from God our Father. I thank my God..." (vs. 1-2, 4)*

People need to feel valued, and when they do, they are more likely to receive what you have to say. Everyone wants to feel significant. In fact, the need for significance is the #1 addiction in America today. When people feel insignificant, they withdraw emotionally and hinder negotiations. If you honor your prospects, they are more likely to respond favorably. Value the people, and they will value doing business with you.

Express value for the people at all levels, not just the "decision makers." A man wanting to make inroads into a huge account sent his introductory letter via next day air. When it was due to arrive, he called the secretary to ask her to personally ensure that it got to the executive he had sent it to. Apparently he didn't express value for her role, making her feel less than competent, because she took offense to his request. She happened to be the wife of the "number two" man in the company, and she made sure the "new guy" didn't make any further progress.

5. Invest in the relationship: *"making mention of you always in my prayers" (vs. 4)*

People don't care how much you know until they know how much you care. How have you invested in the relationship so far? How can you invest in the relationship now? Taking the time to invest in the relationship will limit how many clients you can serve well, but serving customers well is the point, isn't it?

Are you only looking at a transaction for what you can get out of it? Look for ways you can invest in your prospects' dreams, such as sending them relevant articles and referrals. I know of a top sales rep who calls on contractors in hopes of having them send him a certain type of specialized work he knows they can't do themselves. One of the ways he became very successful with them was by first sending them business that his company couldn't provide. In return, the contractors have reciprocated and helped him become very successful.

6. Involve their good reputation: *"hearing of your love and faith which you have... the hearts of the saints have been refreshed by you brother" (vs. 5 & 7)*

Recognize your prospects' past achievements. Maybe they are well-known for their leadership or for resolving difficult situations. It doesn't hurt to remind them that their reputation may be at stake. Proverbs says that a good name is better than great riches. Many people know this and strive to build and keep their good name. Building a good reputation is hard enough, let alone trying to rebuild one. Where appropriate, attach their reputation to the outcome because people want to protect their reputation.

7. Build on past gains: *"beloved friend... fellow laborer... fellow soldier... brother... partner" (vs. 1, 2 & 17)*

Don't re-invent the wheel or lay the same foundation. Reiterate progress made thus far and keep in the forefront the gains or progress you have already made together. Perhaps they have been a customer for a long time. You might want to remind them by saying something like, "You've been a customer a long time now" or "We've worked together before." Customers are hesitant to end a relationship and exchange it for one of unknown quality. If you have had customers for a long time, you might remind them of things like their past service history that your company understands better than anyone else possibly could.

8. Affirm their destiny: *"that the sharing of your faith, may become effective by the acknowledgment of every good thing which is in you in Christ Jesus" (vs. 6)*

Affirming your customers' destiny or sense of purpose will enhance significance. When you recognize people are doing an excellent job, let them know how well fitted they are for that work. If they are doing what they're wired for and you recognize that, it will greatly enhance their own self worth, and when their significance is enhanced, they are more likely to do business with you. This does not mean that you comment on people favorably so you can get their business. Instead, when you recognize their giftedness and how well fitted they seem for the job they are doing, your comments will uplift and encourage them and eliminate any sense of threat from you. When people feel encouraged by your presence instead of threatened by it, they are much more receptive to your message, which increases your chances of doing business with them. Come alongside their business and help them fulfill their destiny.

9. Affirm their positive attributes that you would like to see manifest: *"hearing of your love and faith which you have toward... all the saints... For we have great joy and consolation in your love" (vs. 5 & 7)*

Acknowledge their positive character traits, like promptness, fairness, honesty, etc. Magnify that trait by discussing their use of that quality in the past. Remind them of the fair-handed way they worked with you the last time they evaluated competitive options. When you talk about their positive qualities, they are more likely to purposefully exhibit those traits in the present transaction. Establish those desirable traits as part of the context for doing business together.

10. Affirm their influence for good: *"the hearts of the saints have been refreshed by you brother" (vs. 7)*

People want their lives to count for something good and to leave a mark. Remind them they have the power to do something good at this time. Perhaps their decision can make a lasting positive impact on the entire organization. Let them know they have the power to do something really good. Perhaps you're dealing with customers who are about to retire and who don't want to affect the status quo. Challenge them to do something that is for the good of the company, which will be a reminder of their influence in the company for years to come.

11. Reveal your position of strength: *"though I might be very bold in Christ to command you what is fitting..." (vs. 8)*

Sometimes you need to remind the party you are dealing with that you could act without their approval but it's more important to you to have a long-term, working relationship. For example, suppose there is a collection issue where they owe your firm for past services rendered. You might need to remind them that you have the upper hand in that situation but are more interested in a speedy resolution and working together in the future. It could be something as simple as, "Our agreement only calls for X, but in the interest of a long-term relationship . . ."

A businessman once owed me money for a piece of office equipment. He finally sent me the agreed upon amount, but the check he sent didn't clear the bank. When I called, he offered to replace it, but never mailed another check. I extended him any terms he felt comfortable with. He finally sent a second check of a lesser amount, but it also bounced.

By this time, I was getting a little frustrated, not because I hadn't gotten paid, but because each promise of payment had been broken. I revealed my position of strength by reminding him that the checks he had written and bounced now constituted a felony offense. I went on to explain that I didn't want to injure him and I preferred to find a solution that he could commit to and honor. I was willing to let him set the terms as long as he honored them. He responded favorably and within hours made good on his check.

12. Base your appeal in humility: *"yet for love's sake I rather appeal to you - being such a one as Paul, the aged" (vs. 9)*

Paul commanded the attention of kings, but humbled himself anyway. People tend to resist a prideful spirit or forcefulness and will look for a way out of the negotiation if it gets too uncomfortable. When you walk in humility and the fear of the Lord, God promises riches, honor and life (Proverbs 22:4). When you walk in humility, I believe God gives you the grace and ability to successfully pass through each set of negotiations.

An appeal is better than force, but don't let the other party see that as weakness. That's why you need to reveal your position of strength and walk in humility. Teddy Roosevelt said it best, "Walk softly and carry a big stick!"

13. Appeal to their good nature: *"being such a one as Paul, the aged, and now also a prisoner of Jesus Christ" (vs. 9)*

It's okay to be vulnerable. Paul revealed his disadvantages: being old and a prisoner. His vulnerability could be easily taken advantage of, but Paul took the risk because he knew the kind of man Philemon was.

In sales, it's okay to reveal vulnerability. No product can be everything to all people. Freely admit the limitations of your product or service and then offset them with the compensating strengths you have to offer. People trust people who are willing to admit their limitations, but suspect and resist those who are not willing to reveal the limitations of their offering.

14. Clarify the topic of concern: *"I appeal to you for my son Onesimus" (vs. 10)*

Paul makes it clear that he wants to talk about Onesimus. He has set the stage and laid the groundwork. Now he is ready to discuss an issue that no doubt is a sensitive one.

When you have a sensitive issue to talk about in sales, whether it is price, delivery schedule, or something else, be direct. It implies importance and minimizes misunderstandings. If you hedge about the topic of concern, your customer will also want to back away from it and agreement will be harder to come by.

15. Redirect opinion with well-chosen words: *"my son Onesimus, whom I have begotten while in my chains" (vs. 10)*

This is the central and most powerful negotiating skill revealed in Paul's letter. He shapes the argument with his words by referring to Onesimus as "his son." That's a powerful claim, especially considering the fact that Onesimus was not his property and Onesimus was a runaway slave. Paul didn't say, "I want to talk to you about that useless slave of yours who vandalized your property before he left." Instead, he wanted to paint a different image in the mind of Philemon. Paul put the conversation on a whole new level when he claimed Onesimus as his son.

Well-chosen words shape an argument, which is why "used" cars became "pre-owned" cars. It's all in the wording. In sales you talk about the investment for your product or service, not the cost of it. You want customers to authorize the agreement, not sign your contract. Think about it, what image comes to your mind when you think of signing a contract? Words have connections to other ideas. For example, signing a contract may remind someone of the phrase, "sign your life away," which is not the thought you want running through your customer's mind at that critical moment. The Mafia puts out contracts on people and everyone knows what that means, so where possible, avoid using words, like "contract," that have negative meaning. As Dennis Peacock says, "ideas have consequences." Think through your choice of words as you present your ideas for consideration.

16. Express your personal commitment to a successful conclusion: *"my son Onesimus whom I have begotten..." (vs. 10)*

Paul lets Philemon know that he has a personal involvement and commitment in the issue. He wants Philemon to know that it was he, Paul, who personally brought Onesimus to the Lord, and because it's personal, the desire for a successful conclusion is very high.

In sales, make a personal commitment to see the matter through to a successful conclusion. Let your customers know that it matters to you and that you will walk through the entire process with them. Express a personal commitment to a successful conclusion. If it's not important or valuable to you, customers will likely pick up on this and you will probably fail to reach a positive conclusion.

17. Insist the outcome be based on current facts: *"who was once unprofitable to you, but now is profitable to you and to me" (vs. 11)*

Paul established the disadvantages of the previous arrangement, reminding Philemon of how unprofitable Onesimus was to him in the past. He informs Philemon of the new set of facts that Onesimus is now indeed profitable, not only to Paul, but under the proposed arrangement, he will be profitable to both of them.

Perhaps your company came through some difficult times and the competition is slandering you with a bad report. If things have changed for the better, you need to let your customers know that the information has changed. Insist that the outcome be based on current realities, not former ones. Remember that people are reluctant to change unless it's more painful to stay the same, so remind new prospects of the pain of staying where they are and current customers of the pain of leaving.

18. Reveal other available options: *"whom I wished to keep with me... but without your consent I wanted to do nothing" (vs. 13-14)*

Paul could have kept Onesimus with him, and he let Philemon know that. Let the other party know you have other options.

A powerful tool in negotiating is having other options. When you sit down to negotiate with a customer and feel like you have to get this sale "or else," you ratchet up the tension unnecessarily. Always be prepared mentally to walk away from the sale. Never sit down at a negotiating table that you can't get up from! Know in advance what your bottom line is and don't cross it. There's always another buyer for your product and most are willing to allow you to make a profit. Take your product or service there. You don't really want a customer who will nickel and dime you to death.

19. Affirm your respect for them: *"But without your consent, I wanted to do nothing..." (vs. 14)*

Paul showed respect by choosing to not do anything without Philemon's consent. He could have taken matters into his own hands, but chose not to out of respect for Philemon.

When you show respect, you earn favor, and favor is exactly the climate you want when proposing new ideas to a customer. If your agreement is reached by manipulation or pressure, it will likely fall apart when tested. Cultivate a spirit of cooperation, not force.

20. Assume a successful conclusion: *"that your good deed might not be by compulsion, as it were, but voluntary" (vs. 14)*

Paul speaks of Philemon's good deed before he has ever agreed to do it. Plant the seed early that you expect to arrive at a successful conclusion. Nurture that idea throughout the negotiations. Acknowledge obstacles, but affirm your conviction of a positive outcome. It will create a positive atmosphere of expectancy.

21. Direct focus to the positive side of negative circumstances: *"For perhaps he departed for a while for this purpose, that you might receive him forever, no longer as a slave, but more than a slave, a beloved brother" (vs. 15-16)*

Paul knew the negative circumstances surrounding the arrival of Onesimus, how he had caused injury to Philemon's property, etc., but he chose to focus on the positive outcome by referring to him as a "beloved brother."

Adversity and opportunity are joined at the hip. Negative circumstances are a passport to something greater. Become a master at discerning the positive side of negative circumstances and causing your customers to see that positive side.

22. Express mutual benefits: *"a beloved brother, especially to me but how much more to you..." (vs. 16)*

Paul didn't mind revealing that he was getting something out of this. He was amply rewarded and wanted Philemon to know it.

Don't be embarrassed to discuss what's in it for both parties. Customers expect that you are getting something out of the agreement also. Most people are leery of the fellow who says he is losing money on the transaction. Of course you'll be well rewarded if the agreement is reached, otherwise you couldn't stay in business and continue offering valuable service.

23. Recall prior covenants: *"If you then count me as a partner..." (vs. 17)*

If you have worked with customers on a project or on solving a problem, build on the strength of past covenants you have previously honored. Remind them of the success you have had working together in the past.

24. Ask for a decision: *"If then you count me as a partner, receive him as you would me" (vs. 17)*

Clarify exactly what you want, then ask for it. When you have made your case and answered their concerns, communicate what the outcome will look like if you move ahead. Paul wanted Philemon to accept and welcome Onesimus with all the love and affection that he would have welcomed Paul himself. Both Paul and Philemon knew what that meant, so Philemon was very clear on what Paul wanted to happen.

25. Plan for the unexpected: *"But if he has wronged you or owes you anything, put that on my account" (vs. 18)*

Paul anticipates a possible objection and nips it in the bud before it can be raised. He expects the unexpected.

You should do the same and prepare to assume responsibility where appropriate. Have a prepared answer for possible glitches. Know what concessions you can make and be ready to offer them if the need arises.

26. Commit to a written contract: *"I, Paul am writing with my own hand" (vs. 19)*

The fact that Paul wrote the letter was purposefully stated for Philemon to see. Paul wanted to emphasize his commitment by putting his request in writing.

When you want prospects to commit in writing, you refer to it as "authorizing an agreement." If you want them to feel secure that you are committed to them, you let them know that you will sign a written contract. It implies you cannot withdraw and that you would not even entertain the idea. Always clarify your verbal agreements in writing. Verbal contracts have destroyed many relationships.

27. Provide logical justification: *"I will repay, not to mention to you that you owe me even your own self besides" (vs. 19)*

Paul provides a little cost justification by reminding Philemon that he owes Paul far more than Onesimus owes Philemon.

Sometimes your customers need a little logical cost justification to help settle the matter. Perhaps Philemon was willing to receive Onesimus but knew that his wife was still reluctant. He could now say, "but I owe Paul my life, how can we turn his request down?" Make it easy for your prospects to say "yes."

28. Appeal to their motivational gift: *"the hearts of the saints... been refreshed by you... refresh my heart in the Lord" (vs. 7 & 20)*

By recognizing that Philemon had the gift of refreshing others, Paul asked Philemon to refresh him. People usually rise to the level of expectation you have of them, as long as it's clearly understood. If your contact at a customer's office is a problem solver, and you're trying to get buy-in within the organization, let your contact know what a good problem solver he is and how confident you are in his ability to get buy-in from others.

29. Express confidence that they will do the right thing: *"Having confidence in your obedience... knowing that you will do even more..." (vs. 21)*

The expectation you project is the expectation the customer will take on. If they sense your confidence, it will generate more confidence. If you approach with the possibility they'll refuse you, it multiplies the likelihood of that happening.

30. Project an ongoing relationship based on a successful outcome: *"But meanwhile, also prepare a guest room for me..." (vs. 22)*

Talk beyond the point of agreement. Discuss what the situation will look like after the equipment is installed, the policy is in place, or the service has been rendered. Talk about the future as though it was already agreed upon. You might say, "What other department would benefit from sales training?" or "Once this is up and running, what are you going to want us to do with old equipment?"

Paint a vision of what the future will look like after the agreement has been consummated.

31. Make it easier to agree than to disagree:
"prepare a guest room for me... Epaphras, my fellow prisoner in Christ Jesus greets you, as do Mark, Aristarchus, Demas, Luke, my fellow laborers" (vs. 22-25)

Involve others whose opinions matter. Paul lets Philemon know who is watching for the outcome at his end. He wants Philemon to know that whether or not he chooses to reveal this letter to others, there are plenty of mutual friends who have an interest in the outcome who are already "in the know" about this letter.

Are there others you may want to be involved in your process who are not directly related to the outcome? Mutual acquaintances at the country club? Your bottom line is that you want to make it easier for customers to agree than to disagree.

16

Finding Purpose in Your Profession

Self-motivation is simply providing yourself with a motive to take action. When you're not motivated, your activity declines, your skill deteriorates and your principles have little to empower. Finding fresh motivation can be a challenge, but depending on others to provide it is far worse. The great patriarchs of the faith possessed great motivational habits.

Driven by destiny

Think of how incredibly difficult it would be to be kidnapped as a teenager and sold into slavery.

Imagine being falsely accused of a crime and being sent to jail for years. Joseph of the Bible endured these and other hardships, never wavering on his belief that God had a destiny for him. He looked at his present circumstances as a training ground for his destiny. He considered the evil done to him and said, "What was meant for evil, God intended for good, to save many people" (Genesis 50:20). He knew he had a destiny and he never let go of that, even through his darkest hours.

When I was seventeen, I lived in Vancouver, British Columbia. A friend of mine invited me to a party in Calgary, Alberta, a mere six hundred and fifty miles away. The legal drinking age was lower in Alberta, so I thought I might be able to purchase my first alcohol. We drove to Calgary in my mother's Toyota, attended the party where liquor was flowing and no one cared how much you drank. My friend Dale and I agreed that whoever got the most incapacitated did not have to drive, and seeing as how neither one of us was interested in driving, it became rather competitive. Being a novice at alcohol consumption, I won the competition and was soon fast asleep in the back seat of the car as my friend began the twelve-hour drive home.

Around 6:30 the next morning, I volunteered to drive for a while. Dale quickly fell asleep in the passenger's seat while I drove, but I soon found myself groggy and fighting to stay awake. To help stay alert, I kept the car going at a high rate of speed (not very smart!). As you would expect, I fell asleep at the wheel.

I opened my eyes as we were flying over about a fifty-foot embankment at a speed estimated by the police to be around eighty-five miles per hour. My first reaction was to hit the brakes, but as I immediately discovered, they didn't work in the air! Dale woke up when we hit the first boulder and the car began bouncing end over end for nearly a fifth of a mile. We felt like dice in a tin can. Finally the car came to rest at the bottom of the ravine.

We crawled out of a window space and hid behind a rock waiting for the car to explode like in the movies, but nothing happened. We examined ourselves for damage: Dale had two small facial cuts and a slightly sore back, and I had no bumps, bruises or any sign that I had been in a serious car accident. We were both extremely fortunate, but didn't realize it at the time.

After getting examined at a local hospital, we caught a bus the remaining four hundred and fifty miles home. I ended up sitting beside an elderly Christian man who, upon hearing my tale, began telling me that God must have a plan for my life. The man instantly turned me off, but what he said intrigued me. After that, Christians started showing up in my life and telling me that God had a purpose for keeping me alive—and the very idea captured my heart! A few months later, in the privacy of my own bedroom, I sincerely asked God to forgive me for trying to live my life my way and asked Him to do whatever it was that He did to people. I expected nothing, but got everything. His presence filled my room and my heart as He lifted my sins off my shoulders and filled me with His grace and His mercy. I knew something happened but I couldn't articulate it. I knew there was a God and that I had been created with a purpose and I knew I would find it.

Ten principles of destiny

Principle 1- Everything under heaven has a purpose

If you were created, then there was a design, and if there was a design, then there has to be purpose. Since there are no two people alike, it's reasonable to surmise that no two people have the same exact purpose or destiny. Creation implies purpose. Our mission is to find that purpose and live it out. There is a purpose in your present circumstances just as there was purpose in Joseph's.

Principle 2 - Sometimes purpose is unknown

We all know people who don't have a clue as to their destiny or purpose in life. They have never really considered the proposition, but their ignorance is not the end of the story.

Principle 3 - Just because you don't know your purpose doesn't mean there isn't one

Many people don't know the purpose of getting further education, so they don't go to college or vocational school. That doesn't mean there is no purpose in further education, they just haven't discovered it yet. Similarly, many don't see the purpose in their present job situation, and as a result, hop from one job to the next, never really mastering anything. Others see their job merely as a paycheck and miss out on the much larger picture. There is much more to life!

Principle 4 — Where purpose is not known, abuse is inevitable

Give a perfectly good gasoline engine to a sixteenth century fisherman and he would thank you for the new anchor. Abuse is inevitable when you don't understand purpose. In the first blood transfusion on record, a man was given sheep's blood in one arm while draining his old blood out the other. When the transfusion was done, he felt wonderful and bought all his friends a round of drinks at the tavern. Then he keeled over and died! The doctors didn't know the unique properties of human blood and they inadvertently abused the patient's body.

When you don't understand your purpose or destiny, you will inadvertently abuse your life. You might be successful by some standards in that you might acquire wealth and fame, but it will be an empty box with a very dark place inside. You need not look far to see the lack of purpose or meaning in merely acquiring things.

In 1923, some of the most successful men of their time met at the Edgewater Beach Hotel in Chicago. The list included the president of the largest independent steel company, the president of the largest utility company, the greatest wheat speculator, the president of the New York Stock Exchange, a member of the President's Cabinet, the greatest "bear" on Wall Street, the head of the greatest monopoly, and the president of the Bank of International Settlements. These men were envied throughout the world for their wealth.

Twenty-five years later, a nosy reporter decided to see how these men had finished their race. He found that Charles Schwab, founder of the largest independent steel company, lived on borrowed money the last five years of his life and died broke. Samuel Insull, president of the largest utility company, died penniless in a foreign land, a fugitive from justice. Arthur Patton, the greatest wheat speculator of his time, died financially destitute in a foreign country. Richard Whitney, president of the New York Stock Exchange, had served time in Sing Sing Federal Penitentiary. Albert Fall, member of the President's Cabinet, was released from prison so he could die at home. Jesse Livermore, the greatest "bear" on Wall Street, Ivar Kreufer, head of the world's greatest monopoly, and Leon Fraiser, president of the Bank of International Settlements, all ended their illustrious careers with suicide. Regardless of the great heights a man may achieve, without a God-given sense of destiny, abuse is inevitable.

Principle 5 - Your destiny is the result of your character

The choices you make are made from your character. People of poor character will typically make poor choices, which will have an adverse effect on them finding and fulfilling their true purpose and destiny. Poor choices in the present moment can limit good choices in the future. My wife spoke with a beautiful young mother who was serving time for a drug-related offense. She happened to be on a boat with some friends who were transporting some illegal drugs. She was not a drug dealer or a drug user and was just along for the ride, but when the Coast Guard found drugs on board, she was sent to prison for ten years without the possibility of parole (the others received harsher sentences). She made one poor choice to hang out with some questionable friends under questionable circumstances and for the next ten years her choices were for the most part made for her.

Principle 6 - Your character is the result of your habits

Develop the habit of consistently doing the right thing. It will strengthen your character, and good habits can be some of your best friends, while poor habits can be some of your worst enemies.

Principle 7 - Your habits are the result of your individual acts

Make quality individual decisions. Each individual choice you make contributes to the establishment or destruction of a habit. If it indeed takes about twenty-one days of consistently doing the same thing to establish a habit, then start now. If you find you have some bad habits, focus on the individual act that contributes to the habit and gain victory over that action. When you successfully make quality individual choices, you will soon find yourself with quality success habits.

Principle 8 - Your acts are the result of your thoughts

What are you thinking about? Someone once said, "We have never committed a visible act of sin that has shamed us before others that was not first a shameful thought." The thoughts we dwell on will sooner or later manifest themselves in some visible expression of that thought.

Principle 9 -   Your thoughts are yours to choose

The good news is that you are free to choose your own thoughts. You can bring every thought captive to the obedience of Jesus Christ (II Corinthians 10:5). You have been given the freedom to choose, so use it wisely.

Principle 10 -   Choose great thoughts and reap a great destiny

Consider the words of Paul: "Finally brethren, whatsoever things are true, whatsoever things are honest, whatsoever things are just, whatsoever things are pure, whatsoever things are lovely, whatsoever things are of good report. If there be any virtue, if there be any praise, think on these things" (Philippians 4:8).

Nine questions to ask to help you fulfill your destiny in sales

1.   Are you committed to principle-based, integrity-oriented selling?

If you are not committed to quality, principle based choices, you will only dream of your destiny. You won't actually walk it out.

2.   What is in your heart?

Psalms 37:4 says, *"Delight yourself in the Lord and He will give you the desires of your heart."* What has God deposited in your heart?

Many feel called to the pastoral ministry but feel they are languishing in a sales job, not discerning the excellent preparation a career in sales or another service field can be for the pastoral ministry. Whatever your calling, don't minimize the necessary period of training.

3.   What stirs passion in you?

It was said of Jesus after he took a whip to those selling goods in the temple that the zeal of the Father's house has *"eaten him up"* (John 2:17). He had an incredible zeal for the house of God and for the people who were looking for God in His house, and His passion was evident to all. Ask yourself what stirs passion in you? What injustice or wrong really stirs you up? What do you talk about? It might be a clue to your destiny.

4.   What flows naturally with your talents?

Are you good at math? Do you understand electrical theory? Can you carry an interesting conversation? Are you more comfortable with concepts? Whatever you like to do, you need to find a line of work that flows naturally with your talents. Few are born with natural selling talent. When I started in sales, I was so petrified of making a presentation to a group of more than one that I always had my boss do them. One day, he cut me off from his support and I was left to sink or swim on my own. One quality I did possess was the ability to put thoughts together in a cohesive manner, but did not have the skill to sell. I lacked the confidence to speak to a group of two or three, but it was a skill that I learned. Look at what flows naturally with your talents and gravitate in that direction. But don't make the mistake of saying you are not cut out for sales just because you are not doing well or enjoying it. Anything worth doing is worth doing poorly! If succeeding in sales is worth doing, then it's worth going through the pain and misery of having to first do it poorly—until you can do it well! If you keep at it, you will eventually succeed. My first year in sales, I barely made a living. My second and third years were much better, and then it took off from there.

5.   What flows naturally with your background?

What has life prepared you for so far? Moses spent forty years on the backside of the desert, tending sheep. He knew how to deal with stubborn animals and God was going to use that experience to lead His people through the wilderness for another forty years. What have you been through that can be used to hasten you in the direction of your destiny?

6.   Are you learning from seasoned professionals?

Do you know someone who can mentor you in an integrity-based approach to the selling process? Learn from the experienced professionals around you who operate in a principled manner. Don't spend your time learning from those whom you do not trust.

7. Are you satisfied with your profession?

Sometimes dissatisfaction is a result of poor sales results. Don't mistake a selling slump for an indication that you need to be in another career. Perhaps you are selling a product that you've come to believe is not in people's best interest to acquire. If that's the case, find something you believe in, then sell it with gusto. If the only way to make sales in your profession is to misrepresent your product, then change companies, products, or your profession. Sometimes you simply need to change your outlook. Instead of firing yourself, get fired up! I once met a man who told me he was "peddling" insurance. He was obviously unhappy with his profession, so I suggested that he do himself and his boss a favor and find a different line of work.

8. Are you getting maximum advantage from other members on the team?

You are part of a team. To succeed in sales, it's better to work with the team members instead of against them. Perhaps the other team members are in non-sales positions, but they may still be able to contribute to your success. Make sure you are getting maximum advantage from all the other team members.

9. Are you faithfully discharging all your current responsibilities?

If you're not faithfully discharging your current responsibilities, there's a good chance you're not ready for the next challenge. Jesus said, "You have been faithful over a few things, I will make you ruler over many things" (Matthew 25:21).

Master the task at hand. Excel more than your peers and you will be first in line for the next promotion or opportunity.

Principle 11 - Lack of destiny will leave you stagnating in the pond of mediocrity

You might do an average job, but if all you want is average, you won't be ready to go to the next level. A sense of destiny will pull you out of the pond of mediocrity every time. You might not know all there is to know about your destiny, but that's okay. Lean into your destiny! You'll find yourself walking in your destiny before you know it.

Principle 12 - A sense of destiny will carry you through the difficult times

David knew he would be king, but until God placed him on the throne, he refused to make it happen his own way. He had the opportunity to kill Saul, who had been ruthlessly pursuing him, but instead he waited patiently on God. He held together through the hardship because of his sense of destiny.

The hard times will eventually pass, but in the mean time, use the challenging times to prepare your character and heart for what lies ahead. When you lean into your destiny, you will find yourself living into your destiny, which will in turn carry you through many a storm!

17

Opportunities Are Guarded
by Problems

Albert Einstein said, "In the middle of difficulty lies opportunity." This principle of opportunity knocking at the least likely moment is something that must be learned by firsthand experience. You can take someone's word for it, but when it happens to you, it's a revelation that you will never forget.

Opportunity 1 — Every situation, properly perceived, becomes an opportunity

Did you hear about the employee who used to walk his dog in the woods? By the end of the walk, the dog's fur would be full of burrs, stuck securely in the tiny hairs. One day he looked closely at the annoying little burrs and saw something truly inspiring. As a result, he invented what we now call Velcro!

Another employee apparently had a bad day in the glue factory and had made up what everyone thought was a bad batch of glue. The problem was that it had only marginal stickiness. A little thought into the matter and "sticky notes" were born!

Another gentleman, who sold potato chips to grocery store chains, was having marginal success in getting the stores to allocate much shelf space for his product. One day his daughter came home from school with her science project. She had to go in the forest and collect leaves from the various species of deciduous trees, and when she returned, she had the leaves neatly stacked one upon the other. It gave him an idea that would change the balance of power in the potato chip wars. He came up with the idea for stacking potato chips in a can. The cans took up less space than bulky bags filled with air and he was able to get more product in the smaller space than his competition. The wave of Pringles was born!

Opportunity 2 — Improving skills removes barriers, while shifting paradigms moves mountains

You can wait for something to come along to shift your paradigm, but chances are you won't like it, or you can artificially shift your paradigm to help you see other options. Though some artificial shifting of paradigms may appear silly to some, the effects are helpful.

For example, when I was selling copiers I would sometimes ask myself what I would do if I got a call from a kidnapper who had kidnapped my wife. I would then tell myself that the ransom was that I would have to sell another copier by the end of the day and it had to be within normal profit margins and no one could know about the kidnapping. Failure was not an option, so I came up with prospects who I hadn't thought of in months and other opportunities that might be worth pursuing. I would then go after those opportunities like my life depended on it, and regardless of whether I made a sale that day, I got myself out of any ruts and started the pipeline moving again. Try shifting your paradigms artificially. You might be surprised what you come up with.

Five characteristics of an eagle-like perspective

Not only can eagles see things clearly from great distances, but due to their positioning, they have a completely different perspective than do land animals. Our perspective must be clear and from the right angle.

Characteristic 1 — Long range

There was a young lad who loved to draw. Everywhere he went he carried his pencil and paper and drew whatever caught his fancy. One day, an elderly gentleman asked him to draw a picture of a horse. When he finished his drawing, the man gave him a dollar. The young lad was greatly encouraged and in a few more years, landed a job at a Kansas City newspaper as a cartoonist. He was very pleased with himself, but the editor called him into his office one day and gave him some unsolicited career counseling, suggesting he find another line of work where he would have a chance to succeed. "After all," the editor remarked, "you don't have any talent."

The young man chose to continue his cartoonist career and eventually came up with an idea that would require a substantial investment. He applied for a loan at three hundred and two different places, but none thought he had the talent to pull it off nor a strong enough idea to ensure a payback of the loan, but he kept on with his dream. He was thinking long-range. Then finally a bank agreed to the loan, and Walt saw his dream of Disneyland come to pass. And the editor who discouraged Walt from pursuing his destiny? Nobody even remembers his name.

Characteristic 2 — Be focused

There is tremendous power in being focused and remarkable lack of power by being slightly out of focus. When I was young, I used to sit in the summer sun near an ant hill with a magnifying glass. When the ants would come and go, I would try to focus the sun's rays in a highly focused beam of light directly on an ant. If I was slightly out of focus, the ants didn't seem to notice the extra light or heat, but if I was perfectly focused on them with the light, they would be zapped in an instant and turn into a little puff of smoke.

I learned that by being highly focused on an objective, I could achieve amazing results. To get certain projects done, I sometimes shut out everything else and focus only on the task at hand. In sales, you can use this principle by focusing blocks of time on specific sales related activities, such as prospecting, writing proposals, returning calls, etc.

Characteristic 3 — Be long-term

We tend to think of a five-year plan as long-term, but it isn't. I heard of an old church in Europe that was built with magnificent beams from rare old trees. They had estimated the beams would need replacing in about five hundred years, so they planted a grove of the same kind of trees to be ready to harvest in another five hundred years. When it came time to replace the beams in the early 1900s, someone found an old set of plans with hand-written notes revealing the whereabouts of the ancient grove of trees. Sure enough, when they went into the forest, they found the trees and were able to replace the old beams.

When you think about your career, think past the next five years and think about your legacy and your children's children. It will inspire something beautiful in you.

Characteristic 4 — Rise above the storm

Eagles often fly into a storm to catch and ride the strong winds up until they are well above the storm. They use the turbulence to propel them above their circumstances. There's no getting around the fact that life will deal you some storms.

One successful boat builder said, "I build all my boats for a storm." Expect the storm, prepare for the storm, and when it comes, ride the turbulence to a higher place in God. I believe every adversity comes with an equal or greater opportunity. They are in fact joined at the hip. You can't avoid adversity, so embrace the opportunity it brings with it.

My wife and I used to own a small publishing company with only one book title when we ran into a storm that threatened to sink us. We were about to go back to press with a leather-bound version of our book when the only pre-sold book printing deal we had fell through. We had based the entire print run on the amount that was now not going to arrive. We were devastated. We had a tremendous opportunity with potential book sales, but all I could only see was the problem. We prayed that we would see the huge opportunity that had to be connected to the huge problem. By the end of the day, we decided to keep the print run, but instead of leather, we tried a paperback version, which went on to be a huge success for us, yielding a much better profit margin and higher overall sales. Whenever you are faced with adversity, there is an opportunity waiting to be discovered if you have the courage to look for it.

Characteristic 5 — Be self-renewing

Eagles have a mid-life crisis of sorts. They get a calcium deposit built up on their beaks and have to chip off the deposits by smacking their beaks against rocks. During that time, they go through a molting process and something close to depression as they temporarily lose their luster for life. After they go through this change, their strength is renewed and they soar again. We all go through times when we lose some of our luster for living. We must learn how to be self-renewing. Break off your old limiting habits, learn new ways to do things, expand your education, and renew yourself.

Opportunity 3 — The bigger the problem, the greater the opportunity

My first-born daughter was born with Down's Syndrome and a sizeable hole in her heart. They didn't tell us any of this until we had her home for a few days and being new parents we really didn't know anything was wrong. When I finally found out, I was devastated! It completely took the wind out of my sails. For me, it was especially frightening because it was the only thing that I knew I feared might happen to me, and it did.

Suddenly, I was a parent of one beautiful but handicapped little baby girl. Early one morning I laid her on the living room floor and just looked at her while I asked God for His perspective on things. Immediately I realized that God loved me regardless of my level of perfection, or lack thereof. He loved me unconditionally and I had no right to do any less for my daughter. Second, I realized that this trial felt as though someone had taken a backhoe and dug a huge hole in my heart. I knew the hole would fill with water. The question for me was, "Am I going to let it make me bitter or make me better?" I chose the latter. I believed that the adversity had the potential to give us wisdom beyond our years if we would embrace the package it came in. So I embraced my little one and cherished each and every day of the eighteen months we had her. She died six days before Christmas in 1979 and great was the loss of her beautiful life.

Opportunity 4 — You rarely exceed your own expectations

I often tell salesmen not to let their company limit them with their sales quotas. Always set your own expectations and reach for those. The copier company I worked for used to have a sales quota of four units per month, though the national average was 3.2 per month. I set my goal for twenty units per month, and though I never hit it, nobody ever got upset with me for selling twelve to sixteen copiers in a month. Before my first year was over I was asked to be the new sales manager, so I never got to hit my goal and often wished I had stayed on a little longer just so I could have hit that goal.

Another example was Jesse Owens in the 1936 Olympics in Berlin. He was going for a world record and a gold medal in the long jump. On his first attempt he committed a foot fault and had to try again. He committed a similar fault the second time and only had one more opportunity to jump. He slowly walked down to where he would need to land to win the gold medal and placed a red scarf on the sand, then slowly walked back to the starting point.

Unbeknownst to him, his coach kicked the scarf a foot further. Jesse took a good run and jumped without committing a foot fault, landing right on the scarf, a full foot further than was necessary to win the gold and set a world record. I can't prove it, but I bet he would have landed on the scarf if his coach hadn't of moved it because you rarely exceed your own expectations.

Opportunity 5 — Others see us the way we see ourselves

When the twelve spies returned from their reconnaissance mission in Canaan, ten of the spies were spooked by the giants and said, "We were like grasshoppers in our own sight and so we were in their sight" (Numbers 13:33). They saw themselves as grasshoppers, so the people of the land saw them that way too! If you walk into a room with a low self-esteem, others will pick up on it and view you in the same way. If you see yourself as a confident, successful individual, others are more likely to see you in the same light also. Learn to see yourself the way God sees you. If you don't know how He sees you, consider what He did for you in the work of the Cross. You will find that the Father has a profound love for you and created you with a destiny. Get a hold of that and carry that perspective into the day!

18

Live Strategically

Strategic, by definition, is big picture thinking. It is large-scale and long-range in nature, but it must be lived out in the tactical here and now. A great example of strategic planning and tactical living was Noah and the building of the ark. It's the epitome of long-range planning as it took one hundred and twenty years to complete the project and it would impact the future course of recorded history. It definitely qualifies as large-scale, due to the dimensions of the boat and the number and variety of its occupants.

The account of Noah receiving instructions from God for building the ark serves as an extraordinary model for strategic planning.

Strategy 1—Evaluate the Situation *"So God looked upon the earth, and indeed it was corrupt..." (Genesis 6:12)*

· Research the situation—Before proceeding in any endeavor, do your homework! Check things out for yourself. When I was very young and had more desire than brains, I sent a man I barely knew to check out a business opportunity. Based on the strength of his report, I committed myself to a business, which I knew little about. It turned out that the information he provided was deliberately falsified by him to provide himself an opportunity. It took years for me to financially recover from that.

· How thoroughly have you investigated the problem or opportunity you wish to address?—Don't rely just on one source. One credible source is still only one view. It's better to have your information confirmed through multiple sources than to put all your eggs in one basket, only to find out the basket has a broken handle.

· Make sure the information you base your decision on is accurate—If you are unsure that your information is accurate, make generous allowances for error or don't proceed at all. I was asked to do a business seminar in Central America. I hesitated because of the expense involved and because I didn't think there would be much return on investment. I was told that my perception was inaccurate and that the country I was to hold the seminar in had more BMW's per capita than any nation on earth, except Germany. I was quite surprised by this information and it encouraged me to proceed. Upon arrival, I discovered that although there were a lot of BMW's in the country, most of them were old and falling apart. The information I had been given was not accurate and the marketplace was indeed not ideal for providing a return on investment.

Strategy 2 — Make a Decision *"Behold, I will destroy them with the earth" (Genesis 6:13)*

· You will never have all the facts—It has been said, "In every person's lifetime there comes an opportunity to do a very special thing, unique to that person and fitted to his or her talent. What a tragedy if that moment finds the person unprepared and unqualified for that work." You should prepare yourself for opportunity, analyze the facts as you can and accept the reality that you will never have all the information. Sometimes you have to act with less information than you would like. It's hard to know when you have sufficient facts, so get the counsel of others and search the Scripture for any indicators of direction, then make the best decision you can.

· Don't be snared by the "paralysis of analysis"—In the mid-seventies I had an idea for a real estate magazine, which I thought was a superb concept. I analyzed and analyzed and eventually did nothing. A few years later, the concept surfaced in my city and ultimately in cities across the continent. My paralysis of analysis cost me an opportunity. I discovered that "In the valley of indecision, lay the skeletal remains of many a worthy plan." The bottom line to making a decision is this: don't rush and don't delay.

Strategy 3 —Summarize the Vision *"Make yourself an ark of gopher wood; make rooms in the ark, and cover it inside and outside with pitch" (Genesis 6:14)*

· Before God gave Noah the specifics, He gave him an overview—Do you have an overview of where you are trying to go with your life? Moses had a simple overview of his purpose: to "set my people free." Nehemiah had a simple understanding of his primary goal: to "rebuild the wall." Jesus gave an overview of His purpose: to "seek and to save that which was lost." What's the overview of your purpose?

· Is your vision clearly defined?—If you can't outline your vision in 25 words or less, you probably don't understand it. Take time to think through your vision, whether it be your life vision or your vision for a specific project, then try summarizing it on the back of a business card. If you can't do that, it's probably not clear enough.

· Can others read it and run with it?—Ask those who have a stake in your vision if they know what the vision is. See how many people give you the same answer. If you get different answers, you know you're not communicating clearly and it may be because you haven't got it clear in your own mind.

Strategy 4 — Establish the Boundaries *"the length of the ark shall be 450 feet, its width, 75 feet, and its height 45 feet" (Genesis 6:15)*

· Formulate a plan and put it in writing—A goal without a plan is only a dream. When I was new to the selling business, I realized that in order to reach my goals, I would have to accomplish a certain amount of activity. And to accomplish that activity, I was going to have to plan and act differently than I had in the past. I created a simple flowchart of required activity and monitored my progress, knowing that if I did the right things well, I would have the desired result. A simple plan, but it yielded extraordinary results.

· Stay within the sphere of your calling—Not everyone is called to the same position in life, though we are all called to accept the challenge of greatness. Greatness is measured by our service to others. Find a way to outserve your competition and you will be exalted in the marketplace. Let God give you the promotion, not yourself, lest you find yourself promoted to a position of incompetence. When you step outside the sphere of your calling, you step into a realm God hasn't equipped you for and disaster is just around the corner. Sometimes we don't know the boundaries of our calling until we step outside and find ourselves fighting for survival with no backup in sight. God is gracious and patient and will lead us back to the sphere of our calling.

· Don't mistake comfort zone for calling—You may be comfortable in your world right now, but that doesn't mean you are called to remain there. Don't mistake the lack of struggle for the leading of God. In fact, if you're not experiencing opposition, there's a good chance you're headed in the wrong direction! You may be in the center of the sphere of your calling, while simultaneously being in the fight of your life. Without doubt, the Apostle Paul endured much hardship and many trials while functioning within his sphere of calling.

Strategy #5—Define your Strategy *"make a window for the ark... set the door of the ark in its side... make it with lower, second and third decks"* *(Genesis 6:16)*

· Make your plan a series of steps, which taken individually are manageable—Break your plan into bite-size pieces. Many goals or projects seem overwhelming at the beginning. Break them down into their individual components, then break the components down into individual steps that you can see yourself accomplishing.

· Prioritize the steps—Stand back and look at the big picture. Ask God to help you prioritize, then list the steps in the order you will need to accomplish them. Without prioritization, you may find yourself having to redo one or more steps as the project unfolds.

· Identify and implement daily success habits—Ask yourself, "What one thing can I do on a daily basis that would make a tremendous difference in the achievement of my goals?" Think of a few more and begin implementing them. They may be simple things, like proper diet and exercise, or more specific to your sales career like a disciplined regimen of prospecting, practicing your questioning techniques, or choosing to keep better records. Pick anything you want, but always remember to "seek first the kingdom of God and His righteousness and all these things will be added unto you" (Matthew 6:33).

Strategy 6 — Envision the Reward *"I will establish My covenant with you" (Genesis 6:18)*

· Look to the reward—Any dream worth

embarking on and any goal worth pursuing will exact a toll from you. In the challenging times, when you question your own sanity for ever setting out on the path you chose, it helps to remind yourself of the reward of accomplishment. Moses rejected the life of privilege under Pharaoh and chose to suffer affliction with the people of God, esteeming the reproach of Christ greater riches than the treasures of Egypt because he looked to the reward (Hebrews 11:24-26).

· Endure hardships—Just as Jesus endured unspeakable horrors at the hands of those whom He sought to save. He endured it all for the joy that was set before Him (Hebrews 12:2). Don't lose sight of the reward and don't feel guilty about wanting the reward. Consider young David before he became king. He inquired three times concerning the reward for killing Goliath before going out to battle against him. He was told each time that the reward was great riches, the king's daughter in marriage and permanent tax-exempt status for he and his family. This does not mean that these were the only things that motivated David, but they clearly held a keen interest for him, and after killing Goliath, he collected on all three promises.

Strategy 7 — Define your Primary Responsibility *"Go into the ark; you, your sons, your wife, and your sons' wives with you. And... two of every sort... to keep them alive with you." (Genesis 6:18-19)*

· Don't lose sight of your original goal— When you're up to your neck in alligators, it's hard to remember you were there to drain the swamp. In the heat of the battle, you can lose sight of the original purpose or goal. Understand that it can happen and be on the lookout for it.

· Watch out for rabbit trails—This is especially true for visionaries. They rarely see an idea they don't like and it's easy for them to get distracted. Keep your primary purpose your primary focus. Focus on the task at hand and don't look back.

· Avoid worthy-looking but not God-originated tasks—Everyone is offered business deals, many of which seem good, honorable and worthy enterprises, but if they are not part of your life's calling and destiny, don't waste your time. Get rich quick schemes are plentiful, but we must recognize that though our efforts should pay well, money should not be our deciding factor. Diversions will come, so you must do your best to be in the right place at the right time, then you will be ready for a God-originated opportunity.

Strategy 8 — Count the Cost *"take for yourself of all food that is eaten... for you and for them"* *(Genesis 6:21)*

· Determine your investment ahead of time—If you want to succeed in sales, you're going to need to invest time, effort and money in the acquisition and refining of your skills and in doing the things most people won't do that are necessary for success. If you don't count the cost ahead of time, you may be surprised at what is required to succeed and you may turn back. Noah had to calculate the quantity of food necessary for him and all the animals represented on the ark. It was a big and necessary project, for without counting the cost ahead of time, he could have found himself on a ship with a bunch of starving animals!

• Be prepared for possible ridicule—When I told the branch manager that I had a plan to sell thirty-six copiers in the next sixty days (when the sales quota was only eight units), he almost fell out of his chair laughing at me. True, I didn't succeed in that goal, but nobody complained with twenty-four units being sold. When I went ahead with a large print run of my book, the printer thought I was dreaming, but eight months later the books were sold out. If you have a goal that is extraordinary, expect others to ridicule you, especially those who will look bad if you succeed.

• Be prepared to take responsibility for the consequences of your plan being executed — You do your best to count the cost and prepare for the unexpected, but in the end you will be held accountable for your choices. If you attempted more than you were able to achieve, you will only be criticized by those who lack the courage to attempt great things. You will find that those who have attempted great things will not be quick to criticize you. Instead, they will come alongside and instruct you from their experience. Accept their seasoned insight.

Strategy 9 —Begin the Work *"Noah did according to all that God commanded him" (Genesis 6:22)*

• Break the inertia! — No matter how good the plan and no matter how substantial your network of contacts, there will be no result unless you get started. In sales, doing the presentation and writing the proposal can be a lot of fun, but getting the ball rolling with prospecting can be a very different thing. Most sales managers agree that the biggest challenge they have with their sales reps is breaking their call reluctance. Once a prospect has expressed interest, the flow of the call is much easier. To make breaking the inertia easier, set aside a block of time when you will only do prospecting. If you're delaying on taking the first steps in a new venture, set aside a specific time when you will launch out, then commit yourself to that time frame and step out. Most people only talk of their great ideas. You can't steer a parked car, so get out on the road and start driving. And always ask God for wisdom.

  · Get started — The research was interesting, the planning was fun, now it's time to get to work. The most difficult thing for me to do in sales was to cold call, so I would set entire days aside to do nothing but that. After a while, my discomfort with the process and my reluctance to make the next call evaporated. I began to enjoy it. If I had to make twenty cold calls to secure one sale and earn a $500 commission, I would tell myself that each "No" I received actually earned me $25. That put a little pep in my step because I knew there was a direct relationship between activity level and actual results. Soon, I was welcoming the opportunity to cold prospect, but before long, my pipeline filled up and I was spending more time serving customers. My base of customers provided me the leads for new customers and the need for cold prospecting diminished.

When Paul had a vision of Macedonia, he went there immediately. By getting started now, the difficult tasks become amazingly doable. We cannot "monsterize" our problems, as my daughter, Amy, says. We must cut the excuses, face our fears, and slay the monsters in our way.

Strategy 10 — Adjust to Unfolding Details
"take with you seven each of every clean animal, a male and his female; two each of animals that are unclean, a male and his female" (Genesis 7:2-3)

· Your circumstances will change — Noah was originally told to bring only two of every animal onto the ark, but then God told him to bring seven of certain species. Apparently it wasn't a problem, but it was a change. In sales, things are always changing. One day it's a price increase or a new product launch, the next day it's an aggressive new competitor or your territory has been cut. The game is always changing, but the fundamental principles never change. Learn to roll with the changes and adapt quickly. If you don't, you might find yourself replaced by someone who didn't know what the old price was or never had a larger territory. Learn to adjust.

· You will never know everything — It is impossible to know the end from the beginning when you start. If you did know, you probably wouldn't start! The small publishing company my wife and I started is one such example. We had no idea that it required tremendous sums of capital or that the vast majority of new books failed. If we knew how difficult it would be, we wouldn't have started. We had many challenges and we grew through every one of them, and in the process, every book we published was a success, with reprints being necessary on every title. Over ten years later, several titles continue to sell, generating residual income for our family. We even had a couple of books that sold over a quarter of a million copies each! Had I known the risks I know now, I might have missed a great opportunity.

· You can expect the unexpected — Instead of responding to the unexpected with dread, look for the possibilities it represents. You can't prepare for every eventuality, but you can prepare your attitude to handle whatever comes your way. Start now by determining that you will find the opportunity in every adversity. You win either way. Knowing that the unexpected will come and being prepared emotionally for the challenge will better equip you to complete the task.

Strategy 11 — Execute Faithfully *"Noah did according to all the Lord commanded him" (Genesis 7:5)*

· Quitters are forgotten — We remember the name of the first man to climb Mt. Everest (Sir Edmund Hillary), not the name of the first man to attempt it. Nehemiah was remembered not because he got financing to rebuild the wall or because of his lofty position as cupbearer to the king. Instead, he was remembered because he oversaw the building and completion of the wall around Jerusalem. If the wall hadn't been finished, the entire project would have counted for nothing.

· Commitment is required — We must be committed to finishing what we start. Jesus said, "No man, having put his hand to the plow, and looking back, is fit for the kingdom" (Luke 9:62). Resist the temptation to quit half way through. It's one thing to aim for a goal and miss it. It's quite another to start out towards a goal and then turn back.

Strategy 12 —Share the Reward with Others *"God blessed Noah and his sons and said to them, be fruitful and multiply and replenish the earth" (Genesis 9:1)*

· Never forget the Source — It is God who gives the power to obtain wealth (Deuteronomy 8:18) He provides the talent and the opportunity. It's our job to use the talent He has given us on the opportunity (which may be disguised as a problem) He has put before us and to trust Him for the outcome. His purpose in helping us obtain wealth is to establish His covenant on Earth. I don't pretend to understand all the ramifications of that, but one thing is clear: it does include feeding the hungry, clothing the naked, helping widows and orphans, and spreading His gospel to all the world. Think of God as an investment banker and ask yourself what it is about your plan that benefits His agenda? Why should He get excited about your project? What's in it for Him?

19

Build Your Confidence

There's no easy way to acquire confidence. It's not something you are born with and few parents raise their children with the intent of creating confidence in them. But without confidence, we tend to shrink back from opportunity. We fear failure and gravitate to our comfort zones, where risk is small and rewards are few. Confidence is nothing more than an inner conviction about the outcome of a given situation. Similarly, self-confidence is the inner conviction that you have the ability to deliver or perform in that given situation.

Where does confidence come from? How can you know with conviction that you can perform well in any situation? There's no one answer to the question, but the following confidence builders have proven highly effective for increasing confidence.

Confidence builder 1 — Fear God

Strong confidence comes by fearing the Lord (Proverbs 14:26). When you're afraid of God, you run from Him, but when you fear God, you run to Him. And when you get in His presence, you worship Him in humility, realizing He is God and you are not. As He reveals more of Himself, you feel ten feet tall and bulletproof. When you get a revelation that the same Spirit that raised Christ from the dead dwells in the heart of every believer, it will really strengthen your confidence! As Jesus said, "with God all things are possible" (Matthew 19:26).

Confidence builder 2 — Do what you fear

Cold prospecting is one of the hardest things for sales-people to do. It is what they fear the most. The quickest way to overcome that fear is to set aside time to do nothing but cold call. Making yourself do what you fear may not work the first time you try it, but if you keep at it, you will have that fear licked!

Generally speaking, confidence keeps an even pace with ability, so as you push yourself to do the thing you're not good at, you will improve as you go and your confidence will soar. My father was afraid of the dark when he was a boy. He decided one day to overcome that fear, so he waited until his parents were gone from the home, then he went into the windowless basement and sat in a chair in the middle of the room with the lights off. At first, he was terrified, imagining all kinds of things that may have been lurking in the dark. After about thirty minutes of nothing happening, his anxiety eased a bit and after about two or three hours, he was not only unafraid, he was getting bored. That day, at eight years of age, my dad conquered his fear of the dark and learned something that served him well over the years.

Nearly twenty years ago after burying my first-born child, losing my marriage, and failing in a business venture, I found myself with no assets and hundreds of thousands of dollars in debt. I fell back on my sales career, but was terribly lacking in self-motivation. One weekend I attended a sales training seminar at a ski resort where you worked part of the day and skied part of the day. Not being a skier, I rented cross-country skis and headed up the nearest mountain to ski down it. I fell so many times coming down the mountain that I put up my skis for the rest of the day. Later that night as I was walking across a mostly frozen lake, I was struck with the weight of all my problems. They felt like weights on my shoulders, threatening to push me through the ice. In desperation, I called out to God and swore out loud that God permitting, I would not give in to those problems but that I would fight them and conquer them with God's help. I felt like I imagined David felt when he faced Goliath – determined to fight and win but utterly dependent on God for the outcome! I, however, didn't have a slingshot!

The next day I saw the real mountain that had conquered me the day before and it was as if it was taunting me, reminding me of the seemingly insurmountable mountain of problems I was facing. I stopped in my tracks, looked at the mountain head-on and said with fierce determination, "I'm coming back here tonight and I'm going to ski down you until I can ski down you blindfolded!"

It was nearly midnight before I had the chance to get to the mountain and I asked my friend to go with me as a witness, though I didn't tell him of my scheme until we got to the top of the mountain. My first attempt to ski down on cross-country skis was a success—not even one spill. We climbed back up to the top and this time I asked him for his black wool scarf. I fastened the scarf over my eyes, positioned myself at the top of the slope and asked him to give me a push to get me started. If you've never skied blindfolded, it's quite a rush, especially for a novice! For me it was incredibly exhilarating. It had absolutely nothing to do with being a daredevil and everything to do with confronting the devils that taunted and challenged me. When I arrived safely at the bottom, the first thought I had was how lucky I was, so I climbed up to the top again and skied down blindfolded one more time just so I would never think that luck had anything to do with it. When I came to a safe stop at the bottom, not too far from a pine tree, I knew God had enabled me to conquer the physical mountain and nothing would stop me with God's help from conquering the mountain of problems that I had previously feared!

Confidence builder 3 — Increase in knowledge, wisdom and understanding

Because confidence generally keeps pace with ability, you need to become an expert in your field. Read more about your product, industry, and the economy that affects it. A man who is diligent in his business will stand before kings (Proverbs 22:29). Before I do a sales training seminar for a company, I will meet with the owners, meet with sales management, interview sales reps and even go out on calls with them so that I have a good understanding of the world they live and work in everyday. What I learn in the process increases my confidence and delivers far more value to the customer. It's a classic win/win proposition.

Confidence builder 4 — Practice the right things

Practice makes permanent, not perfect, so you must be sure to practice the right things. My golf swing is atrocious, but I play so seldom I don't worry about it, but when I do play I re-enforce my poor form and I get better and better at playing poorly. As I only play once every few years, I let the form go and just have fun, but in your profession, you can't afford to do that.

The famed concert pianist, Van Cliburn, dazzled audiences around the world with the grace and ease with which he played complex musical compositions. What few people realized was that even in his later years, he practiced eight hours a day, and two of those hours were just doing finger exercises! He practiced the right things diligently and the desired results followed.

Confidence builder 5 — Change your self-image

You never rise above your image of yourself. Your reality (what you experience in life) tends to follow self-image. It's okay to realize that you are not the absolute best in your field, but don't get comfortable with your position. Continue to press on, realizing that God loves you the way you are and that He delights in you and takes pleasure in your prosperity (Psalms 35:27).

When I excel in something, I am showcasing some of God's handiwork and I'm only too happy to acknowledge His greatness in the design and implementation of that gift. I know that every good and perfect gift comes from above (James 1:17) and rather than hide my gift, I purpose to work it, develop it, and excel in it so that I might show off the Father's glory and goodness in the hopes of introducing others to Him.

Confidence builder 6 — Raise your expectations

We can be as good at sales—or anything else—as we want to be. I could be a better golfer, but I choose not to invest the time and effort because it doesn't have sufficient payback for me. Instead, I spend time working on being better at what I do.

Even our walk with God is up to us. He promises to meet those who seek Him early and to draw close to those who draw close to Him. How often do we set the time aside just to draw close to Him? My point isn't to make you feel guilty about anything, but to cause you to put the responsibility for most of what you get out of life squarely on your own shoulders. We all experience bad things that we don't deserve and can't avoid, but the responsibility for how we respond to them lies with us. Expect more from yourself than others do. If you expect above average results, you need to expect above average commitment of yourself. Raise the bar on yourself. Don't wait for someone else to do it. If you have a sales quota at work, raise the bar above their expectations. Don't be limited by the company's expectations. Set your expectations higher.

While we are pursuing our goals, let us not allow our priorities to get out of order. The great Scottish essayist and historian, Thomas Carlyle (1795-1881), married his beautiful secretary, Jane Welsh, in 1826. They were quite happy together, but after several years of marriage, she was diagnosed with cancer. Carlyle had become so absorbed with his writing that he had her continue to work at the office despite her ill health. Eventually she was bedridden, but Carlyle was so busy with his career that he barely found opportunity to spend time with her. She died shortly thereafter. Upon returning home from the funeral, he sat down and lamented over how little time he had spent with her when she was alive. While pondering these thoughts, his gaze fell upon the diary Jane kept and he picked it up and began to read. On one page he found, "Yesterday he spent an hour with me and it was like heaven; I love him so." Carlyle had been so busy with his career that he had never noticed how much he had meant to her. He found another page that broke his heart. Jane had written, "I have listened all day to hear his steps in the hall, but now it is late and I guess he won't come today." Devastated by his own neglect of what was truly important, he threw the diary to the floor. His friends found him face down in the mud at the graveside, eyes red from anguished lament, saying over and over again, "If only I had known. If only I had known." But it was too late; she was dead.

When you raise your expectations, raise them on all fronts, not just in your career. Pursue God with a passion, love your spouse deeply, cherish your children, serve your fellow man and find time to rejuvenate. In the time you carve out for your career, push yourself hard, raise your expectations and don't accept excuses from yourself, at least not to the detriment of your relationship with God and your family. No man on his deathbed has ever wished he had spent more time at the office! Give yourself to the pursuit of a balanced life, not to the pursuit of material success alone.

Confidence builder 7 — Build on small successes

Sometimes your goals far exceed your current abilities, and in reaching for them you fall so far short that you're tempted to give up on the whole dream. I met a young man with limited education who got a job selling life insurance. His career path thus far was limited to repairing cars and he barely made enough to keep his family fed. In his first week of selling he explained to me how he was going to make a million dollars in commissions within the next year or so. With almost no training, no discipline and no prior experience, he inevitably fell so far short that he abandoned the sales profession altogether. It was like a three hundred pound, middle-aged man deciding he would win the Olympic gold metal for the high jump with the competition being a week away. That would be ridiculous.

Having lofty goals is between you and God. He did not say that with God all things were probable, he said all things were possible! Miracles do happen, but the rule of thumb is to build upon small successes, "precept upon precept, line upon line, here a little, there a little" (Isaiah 28:10). When I was devastated by personal losses, I struggled to find the motivation just to live, let alone accomplish anything meaningful with my life. A dear friend suggested that I make a point each day of accomplishing something, anything at all, just as long as at the end of the day I could take some satisfaction in having accomplished something. It didn't have to be big—it just had to be accomplished. I took his advice and began developing the habit of daily accomplishing something. Before I knew it, my confidence was growing, the accomplishments were increasing, and my vision for a brighter future was rekindled. Building on small successes is a tremendous way to build your confidence and secure your future.

Confidence builder 8 — Encourage yourself

When David and his men returned from a raid, they found their camp burned and their wives and children missing. David's men were so upset at him that they wanted to stone him, but David separated himself from the people and encouraged himself in the Lord. He likely recalled past successes where God had delivered him. If there's no one around to encourage you, you've got to encourage yourself.

For me, that means I go for a walk and I talk with the Lord. Sometimes I remind myself of the pit He pulled me out of and sometimes I remind myself of His promises. I magnify God and His greatness in my mind, which always dwarfs any problem or challenge I might be facing.

If you need encouragement, take the initiative and encourage yourself in the Lord. It will restore your soul and increase your confidence. When David had encouraged himself in the Lord, he gained the confidence to pursue the invaders who had taken their families captive and he recovered it all!

Confidence builder 9 — Consider not

When Abraham was about a hundred years old, God promised him a son. Abraham did not consider his or his wife's body into the equation. He believed God and took Him at His word. There will always be very good reasons why you can't do something, but all you need is one good reason why you can. People used to believe that if you traveled faster than thirty miles per hour you would suffocate. They were obviously wrong. People had all kinds of "facts" to prove why it was impossible to break the sound barrier, but Chuck Yeager proved them all wrong. In fact, when he crossed the sound barrier, nothing happened inside the cockpit. For him, it was a non-event.

When I first started selling copiers, I asked God to help me arrive at a good goal for my first full month in sales. I wanted it to be high enough to startle the management but within range of accomplishment. Seeing as how I had been told not to expect any sales my first month and only four per month once I got up and running, I thought ten would be an impressive number. On the last day of the month, I had a flat tire on my way to work. When I arrived two hours late at the office, I had a message from my only prospect saying that he did not want to purchase at this time and that I should not call him back. I already had eight sales under my belt for the month, but was two sales short of my goal.

By 2:00 that afternoon, with only three hours remaining in the business day, nothing was clicking. I called my wife for some encouragement. She began to "encourage" me by reminding me that I had already sold eight copiers that month and that I didn't need to put unnecessary pressure on myself. I interrupted her midstream and told her that I loved her but that I couldn't allow her to talk to me like that anymore. I couldn't allow her words to penetrate my heart because I still believed that somehow I could sell two more copiers in the next three hours even though I didn't have any prospects. I couldn't allow her well-meaning words of encouragement to cause me to relax my grip and my focus on the goal. I couldn't afford to consider the reasons I should be satisfied with what had already been accomplished. What I needed to do was put aside all the very sound and logical reasons why it was unreasonable to even think about reaching my goal. But I wasn't into being reasonable. I believed that God and I were working on a goal and I wasn't about to give up on it. I still had three hours.

I actually hung-up on my wife as nicely as I knew how and hoped she would understand. A few minutes later, a man driving by our office saw the sign on our building and pulled in to inquire about purchasing a used copier. He informed me that he wouldn't be buying for several months but wanted to get an idea of what the investment might be. After learning about his needs, I brought him over to a good used copier that he felt perfectly met his requirements. I asked him if he would be interested in the exact same model for the exact same price but with only one tenth of the usage; he answered in the affirmative. I then called the prospect who had told me not to call him and said that I had a customer in our office who wanted to buy the same kind of copier that he had presently and I was wondering if he wanted me to have this customer make the check out to him or us. Essentially, I was offering to sell his used copier for him at retail price, and he asked me to bring the buyer over. When we arrived, the prospect I brought with me agreed to purchase his copier, which of course left my customer with none, so he purchased one from me on the spot. Two sales in three hours! Call it a miracle, coincidence, ingenuity, or whatever, I know it wouldn't have happened if I had considered the reasons why it shouldn't have happened. I believe God looked down on the whole scene, honored my faith, maybe even smiled at my optimism, then out of His grace and kindness sent me the assistance I needed to reach the goal. And yes, the company was suitably impressed and it gave me the platform to glorify Him in a credible way.

Here are eight practical ways to increase your confidence:

1   Enroll in a study course for a topic in which you have interest but no prior training.

2   Take up a new sport or hobby that you have little or no experience in.

3   Find new challenges for yourself in various fields of endeavor, such as physical, intellectual, or spiritual matters and seek to excel beyond past achievements.

4   Find new and creative ways you can be of service to your community.

5   Find new ways you can be of service within your church.

6   Watch less television.

7   Read more books.

8   Make new friends.

20

Implementing the Power of Integrity

In the movie City Slickers, starring Billy Crystal, there was a scene in the movie when he was asked if he would have an affair with a beautiful woman if he knew no one would find out. He insisted that someone would find out, so his friend posed the question a different way. He said, "If a spaceship landed right in front of you and the most beautiful woman you'd ever seen stepped off the craft and offered you sex with the promise that she was going to get back on her spacecraft and leave our solar system forever, and no one would ever know, would you do it then?" Billy Crystal's answer was, "But I would know."

The essence of integrity is living your life by the same principles, whether among rich or poor, friend or foe, or simply in the privacy of your own hotel room while traveling. Who you're with or where you are should no more impact your integrity than last night's ball game impacts today's weather. The truth is that those type of things test what integrity we have and reveal to us what we sometimes don't want to see in ourselves.

Jeremiah said "the heart is deceitful above all things and desperately wicked, who can know it?" (Jeremiah 17:9) We also work out our salvation with fear and trembling (Philippians 2:12) and are a work in progress (Philippians 1:6). We need to raise the standard, to demand more of ourselves than others require, and to reach toward the high calling of a principle centered, integrity oriented lifestyle.

Integrity is "moral soundness" or the quality or state of "being unimpaired." According to surveys of business executives, integrity is the human quality most necessary to business success. Therefore, it stands to reason that we take a closer look at what goes into being a man or woman of integrity.

Integrity Rule 1 — Integrity is not WHAT we do as much as WHO we are

"The first key to greatness," Socrates said, "is to be in reality, what we appear to be." What you do flows out of who you are.

Admittedly, it is very difficult to change what you do unless you can change you first. Work on the inside of you and the outside will take care of itself. The Bible says more about the subject of "being" than the subject of "doing." The word "being" occurs 291 times in the Bible, while "doing" only occurs 39 times. Similarly, the word "be" occurs 7,012 times while "do" only occurs 1,368 times. Clearly, there is much more emphasis on "being" than on "doing." Win the inner private battle for integrity and what you do will not be a problem. Don't focus on the outside symptoms. Instead, focus on being conformed to the image and likeness of the One who created you. The other things that aren't consistent with integrity will drop off you like ice off a hot griddle.

Integrity Rule 2 —Image is what people think we are. Integrity is what we really are

In American business there is an obsession with image. People get caught up in projecting the right image, but often fail to live up to that image. When I was just starting my training and consulting business, a friend offered to represent me in Houston and at the same time I rented a small office in Guatemala to facilitate Latin American seminars. I changed my stationery to include offices in Nashville, Houston and Guatemala City. I wanted that national / international image and it looked good on stationery. However, it projected an image of something we were not—a large, well-established corporation. My venture in Guatemala cost tens of thousands of dollars and knocked me down a few notches.

In addition, the bigger-than-life image required a bigger-than-life budget, so I closed the Guatemala branch and moved the office to our home. The reprinted stationery only had a local post office box for an address. Instead of trying to project an image

I couldn't afford, I told potential clients that if they were looking for a big firm, I could recommend a few, but if they were looking for results, they need look no further. When asked about the size of the "organization," I would tell them I worked alone out of my home. Instead of scaring people away, they were drawn to my authenticity and wanted to know how I could help them. The image I was projecting was in-line with the integrity I possessed and the synergism of the two working together has kept me busy ever since. When the image of your integrity and the integrity you possess are incongruent, you're headed for a wreck and it's only a matter of time before it happens.

The Great Wall of China was originally constructed in the third century and was approximately 1,500 miles long, with an average width of twenty feet and average height of twenty-two feet, and it had forty-foot towers every one hundred yards. It was an impressive structure. The wall was high and thick, and virtually impenetrable, yet it was compromised successfully three times in just the first one hundred years. How did the invaders do it? They bribed the gatekeepers and marched in, unimpeded. The Chinese relied on walls of stone and were undone by hearts of stone. They forgot to teach and model integrity.

Integrity Rule 3 — Through honesty, your words conform to reality

Honesty is an accurate representation of a person, place or thing and involves full disclosure. Communicating by leaving out certain pieces of vital information is not honesty in action.

I once accompanied a salesman on some calls to evaluate his selling style for the owner of the company. On the calls we made, I heard him tell his prospects amazing facts that I didn't know about the company. When I spoke with the owner, I asked him if they really had over a hundred employees; he said they only had about sixty. There were other claims that were also inaccurate, but giving the salesman the benefit of the doubt, I asked him if he knew there were only sixty employees instead of the over one hundred he was claiming. He was aware of the actual number but told me that the fact that he lied to his prospects was my problem, not his. After all, he explained, nobody was getting hurt and he was simply telling them what he thought they wanted to hear.

Truth is always more powerful than a lie. There's something about the feel of it. I can't explain it other than to say that it has weight to it and people can sense it. When you speak, make sure you convey the truth by matching your words to what really happened.

Integrity Rule 4 — Through integrity, reality conforms to your words

This is a little more difficult because we are committing to a future outcome based on some circumstances that may be out of our control. For example, you say you'll be somewhere by eight, but there's a wreck on the interstate and you're stuck for an extra ninety minutes, which makes you late for your next appointment. Barring some unforeseen circumstances, you can keep your word if you want to. Honesty is saying you caught a fifteen pound trout. . . and you really did, while integrity is saying to your son, "I'll take you fishing this weekend," and you really do take him fishing.

Integrity Rule 5 — Charisma will draw people, but only integrity will keep them

A lot of people can talk the talk, but there are far fewer who are willing to walk the walk. I once hired a man to sell books to bookstores across the country. Before committing to the position, he stressed over and over again how important it was to him that we were a company of integrity. I thought he was going to ask us to take a polygraph test! Shortly after he began his employment, his sales started climbing rapidly. Within a couple of months he was selling three to four times what the average rep was selling. We were impressed and gave him an opportunity to call on major accounts. He increased his sales by five times in the first month. It was absolutely unbelievable! Right about then, the orders he had sold six to eight weeks before started coming back. Customers were complaining that they had never ordered the books or they had ordered a much smaller quantity. Soon, a tidal wave of returns made their way back to our shipping department. When confronted with the facts, he looked me straight in the eye and lied through his teeth. In another twenty-four hours his charade was over and he left town in disgrace. His charisma had fooled us for a while, but his lack of integrity caught up with him. I learned that when people stress how honest they are or how much integrity they have, it's an unconscious reinforcement of their own weakness. Actions will always speak louder than words.

Integrity Rule 6 — Integrity is a private victory, not a natural gift

We are all born with a sinful nature. We're selfish and not happy when we don't get our way. As we mature, we learn that we must put aside a dishonest lifestyle if we ever hope to establish anything of value and longevity for our future. Integrity is something we have to work into our lives in a very deliberate and often painful process as we come face to face with the fact that we all want what we want when we want it. Integrity is a victory we win one battle at a time, one choice at a time, and when we do, the internal rewards far exceed any reward we may enjoy on the outside.

21
Steering Your Course with
Well-Chosen Words

In the marketplace, the battle rages over ideas and is fought with the articulate exchange of words. He who expresses his ideas more clearly and more compellingly than his competitor will likely win the battle for limited resources that day. The next day, the competitor will be back with a re-packaged version of what he had yesterday, only better stated, and so the battle wages on.

Words are so simple to utter and so impossible to withdraw. They stir one man to passion and another to despair. They bring life to one man and death to another. Sticks and stones may break your bones, but words can break your spirit. They are invisible containers of spiritual matter that do their work in the soul of man. The battle always begins in the soul with words, then when the words have done their duty, we either beat our plowshares into swords and make war or beat our swords into plowshares and make peace.

We all have a renewable arsenal of words that can either build up or tear down the hearer. Some of the most damaging words you will ever hear will come from your own lips! And because those words are from such a trusted source, you offer little or no resistance. You really have no control over the words someone may speak over you, but you always have control of the words you speak over yourself. When someone speaks words over you that are damning, destructive and not full of grace and truth, you have the duty to not allow those words to find a resting place in your soul. You might ask God if there is anything in those words that bear truth, even if they were meant to be harmful. Wise people can always learn from their enemies as well as their friends.

The words we control are our own, whether they originated with us or with someone else. When we were younger, we probably heard things like "You're stupid," "You'll never amount to anything," and "You're ugly." These replay in our minds to the point that we adopt them as our own words. Then when we are older and need encouragement in a certain area, what we hear ourselves saying are the same hurtful words that we received when we were young.

When I was about eight years old, a school kid I didn't know walked up to me and said, "You're ugly!" and then walked away. I had never seen him before and never saw him again. I reasoned that because he didn't know me, he couldn't have harbored any ill feelings toward me and therefore his words must have been both objective and heartfelt.

When I got home from school, I stood in front of a large mirror and stared at myself in silence. I remember thinking, "So that's what ugly looks like." I believed ugly people had limited opportunities in life, which meant I would never have a girl friend, a wife, or a family. I believed that the sooner I came to terms with that harsh reality and adjusted to life as a loner, the better off I'd be. I probably spent fifteen minutes in front of that mirror thinking through all the ramifications I thought came with being ugly, then I resolved to accept it and deal with it by getting on with my life and lowering my expectations for happiness.

The sad fact is that I grew up believing I was ugly when I wasn't. The school kid's voice became my voice in my mind, and I believed it.

Word choice 1 — As you believe, so you speak

Jesus said, "Out of the abundance of the heart, the mouth speaks" (Luke 6:45). If your heart is full of negative statements or beliefs about yourself, those beliefs will come out in your speech. When you hear yourself say something, either positive or negative, you believe it and reinforce it, so take the counsel of Solomon and "keep your heart with all diligence, for out of it spring the issues of life" (Proverbs 4:23). Find the truth about anything you keep in your heart. If it's false information, get rid of it.

I was told that I was ugly just one time. What if you were told you would never amount to anything over and over and over again throughout the course of your growing up years. It can take a long time to undo such damage. A man once wrote on a 3x5 card the future that God had for him, copied from the Bible. He read those words over and over again, replacing his old words and thinking with truthful words about his destiny. In time he began to believe it and walk it out. He literally became a different person. By continually marinating your mind in the Word, you will come to know the truth and the truth will set you free!

Word choice 2 — As you speak, so you believe

When I was young, I went to the local county fair. I didn't realize that the arcades were rigged, so when I won, the game operator deliberately bumped the table and made it look as though I had lost the game. I was upset and moved on over to the next game, which was one where you threw dimes toward a plate. If the dime landed and stayed on the plate, you won a prize. I kept trying and kept missing. When I got down to my last dime, I threw it ever so carefully, but it failed to stay on the plate, which already had several dimes on it.

Because no one was watching and because I felt cheated from the previous game, I claimed that I had won. The gamekeeper took one look and knew I was lying, but I insisted he was mistaken. My protests went unheeded, so I went home and told my big brothers how I had been cheated at the dime-throwing table, and they went to right this terrible wrong. As I sat at home crying my alligator tears, it suddenly dawned on me that I was crying over something that I knew had never happened. I was stunned by the power of my own words and how I had convinced myself of something I knew to be a lie. I was moved to tears over an injustice that never occurred. I learned to be more careful of the words I spoke in the future because I saw how easily I could hurt myself with them.

We should speak God's truth concerning us and our future. Let those words percolate down into our souls. As they take root in our hearts, belief will spring forth and the words will come back to us again in a harvest of righteous encouragement.

Word choice 3 — As you speak, so you act

People don't like to eat their words. For example, Herod liked John the Baptist, but when he offered his new wife anything she desired, and she wanted John the Baptist's head on a platter, he was unable to back out of his commitment. He was forced to follow through with what he had promised.

When words fall out of your mouth, you tend to follow them, so you need to be very careful of what comes out of your mouth. How many times have you heard, "Well, I've already said it now…" or words to that affect? Proverbs says, "where words are many, sin is not absent" (Proverbs 10:19). Most of us have set our actions in motion by words that we wish we had never uttered. It is never too late to not say what you shouldn't say.

Word choice 4— As you act, so goes your future

The actions you take now set in course an irreversible chain of events that can never be undone. Many of our actions are born out of our words and many of our words are born out of our inner beliefs and so many of our inner beliefs are born out of someone's words planted and engrafted in our soul. It's time we do an inventory of our words and our inner beliefs and plant truth where lies once reigned and nurture that truth with positive affirmation while guarding it from further incursions out of the lips of others who would prefer to see us stay on their level. In short, guard your heart with a passion!

My father told me that there was nothing I couldn't do, and I believed him. I honestly believed that absolutely anything I wanted to do was within my reach and was there for my choosing. The words from my father took root in my young heart and have influenced every part of my life. I realize now that words led to actions, which set me on the course to my destiny. That's simply the way words work.

22

Self-Discipline
The Fruit of Vision

Harry Truman once said, "In regarding the lives of great men, I found that the first victory they won, was over themselves... self-discipline with all of them came first." Self-discipline is choosing to become a disciple to a philosophy, principles, values, or an overriding purpose.

Most of us have a difficult time finding the motivation to exercise much self-discipline in our lives. I spent my entire childhood looking forward to the day when I would be an adult and do "what I wanted to do." When I moved out on my own at age eighteen, I quickly found that the real world was not nearly as free, kind and endearing as I had imagined it to be. Undaunted, I proceeded to keep late hours while working early shifts. "I'm an adult," I said to myself. "I can do what I want." Then one morning on the way to work I fell asleep at the wheel and drove my Volkswagen Beetle straight into the side of a parked semi-trailer. I awoke in the hospital and realized it was time to give up my late nights and start going to bed around the time my parents had suggested. It was amazing how much more alert I was the next day.

I still drove my car the way I wanted to drive it, but three engines and two tickets later, I started driving more like my parents had suggested. It's amazing how smart your parents become the older you get!

For me, the discipline I yielded to was done solely for survival. It was many years later that I learned how to unlock the motivation necessary to push me to do the things I didn't want to do so that I could achieve the things I really did want to achieve. The key is found in Proverbs 18:29, "Where there is no vision, the people perish." The word "perish" is translated in the New King James Version as "cast off restraint." When people have no vision or overriding sense of purpose, they cast off restraint. The key is this: when people have a vision and an overriding sense of purpose, they find the self-will and discipline necessary to accomplish that vision.

Take for example the seven-year old girl who watches the Olympic figure skating competition and decides she wants to become a gold medalist figure skater. She's knocking on her parent's door at four in the morning to get one of them up to take her to the skating rink. She has a powerful vision and the self-discipline necessary to fulfill that vision comes more naturally. On the other hand, if the parents are watching the Olympic figure skating competition and they decide they want their child to become a gold medalist figure skater, they're the ones going into her room at four in the morning and dragging her off to the rink. There's a big difference between the two scenarios.

When you have vision, you work harder and smarter, you track your progress, plan and value time, practice self-improvement, and persevere. In short, you do the things you don't want to do so you can have the things you want to have. When you find that specific vision that provides the motivation to get you going in the right direction, you will still encounter all kinds of resistance to keep you from fulfilling your dream.

Here are ten ways to stay the course:

Course-setter 1 — Recall the original motivational factor

Once you start down the path to your goal, there will be many things that come along to sidetrack you. Some will be opportunities and some will be major challenges you didn't anticipate. You may even want to give up. When that happens, recall the original motivating factor. What was it that got you started? What were you trying to accomplish? Was it a worthy goal when you started? Has that changed? If the original motivating factor is still valid, then you don't need to change the goal, you need to change your attitude about your circumstances and then change your circumstances.

Course-setter 2 — Have quality, achievable goals

One of the biggest hindrances to sustaining motivation is the size of the goal itself. Robert Schuller says, "Inch by inch, anything is a cinch, but mile by mile takes a while." The first rule of goal setting is that your goal must be definable. If you can't define exactly what the objective is and when you must meet the objective, then you don't have a goal, you have a wish. Define your goal.

For example, if in sales you have a goal to earn a certain income, determine when you want to be at that level and how much you will need to sell by that time to earn that income. Then determine what activities you will have to do to make that many sales. This should include prospecting, interviewing, presenting, quoting and closing ratios along with average dollar volume and profit margin per sale. From there you map out how much time the appropriate activities will take and hit the road running.

After a week or so, evaluate yourself and see if you've been able to maintain the activity level you thought was necessary. Then you need to check your ratios. Are you turning enough suspects into prospects? Prospects into quality interviews? Interviews into presentations? Presentations into quotes? Are the quotes averaging the dollar and profit range you predicted? What percentage of your quotes are turning into sales? Don't depend on management to track you. Track yourself! There are a lot of sales reps who don't like the idea of tracking their activities. It is my opinion that those who have no interest in tracking their performance are only interested in having a job, not a professional career with a future. How long do you think a professional baseball player would last on a professional team if he complained that he didn't like being tracked on all his errors and his batting average?

After you clearly define your goals, evaluate them to make sure they are achievable. If you determine that you will have to make one hundred calls to find fifty prospects and engage forty of them in an interview resulting in thirty presentations and thirty quotes of which you need to close at least ten each and every day, you may want to revisit your original goal. Either that or bring in some support to make the preliminary calls so you can spend all your time doing the presenting and closing of orders.

For example, one summer I wanted to win a sales contest selling copiers, so I gave a college kid a summer job working just for me and paid him directly out of my paycheck. Some of the other reps complained that I had an unfair advantage because there were really two of us working in my territory and I had him doing all the busy work while I focused more on the direct customer interaction. Their argument was weak because they could have done what I was doing if they were willing to pay for it. Not too many sales reps are willing to risk their own paycheck to take a chance at increasing sales by enough of a margin to pay for the person they hired and hopefully increase their own earnings. In my case, I had the best three months I had ever had, easily earning enough to pay for him and make a good bit extra besides. Management appreciated my initiative and that autumn made me the sales manager for the region. Once you know your goals are definable and achievable, you must act decisively! He who hesitates is lost. If your goal is well defined with realistic timetables and clearly achievable, don't delay another day. Get started and be decisive.

Course-setter 3 — Envision the pain of failure

Sometimes we don't want the carrot because we are so well-fed, but what we really need is the stick. We all need positive motivation, but occasionally we need to be reminded of the seriousness or consequences of failure.

In 1519, Cortes and some six hundred men landed on the Caribbean side of what is now Mexico. Montezuma, the dread lord and sovereign of all the Aztecs, had heard of their arrival and sent them great gifts of gold and silver in the hopes that they would accept the gifts and return home. Unfortunately for Montezuma, the gifts had the opposite effect as Cortes was now more convinced then ever about the great wealth awaiting them inland. He loaded the gifts of gold and silver on one of their eleven ships and sent them off as a personal gift for Emperor Charles V in hopes of winning the special favor of the emperor. When the ship bearing gifts for the king had departed, Cortes did something absolutely amazing. He ordered that the compasses and gear of the remaining ships be brought ashore, then he ordered all the ships to be scuttled while he and his men watched them sink to the bottom of a placid Caribbean sea. Clearly, there would be no turning back. Their choices were limited to victory or death! Considering the Aztecs outnumbered them by about a thousand to one, it was quite a gamble, but as the ancient Chinese warlord Sun Tzu had claimed nearly three thousand years earlier, "An army that lacked an escape route would fight with the courage of despair." Cortes and his men were seeking fame and riches, but chose an additional motivational incentive: the pain of failure!

Course-setter 4 — Envision the joy of accomplishment

Positive encouragement is a powerful motivator. The thrill of accomplishment far outweighs the tangible benefits that often accompany an accomplishment. When Sir Edmund Hillary was the first to summit Mount Everest, he wasn't expecting, nor did he receive, a cash reward. He was motivated by the thrill of accomplishment. The harder the task, the greater the thrill! Sure, it's nice to win the trophy for being top sales rep, but just being the best is reward enough, though admittedly, the perks of winning are a nice touch!

Course-setter 5 — Draw encouragement out of positive-minded people

Seek out others who are positive-minded and who will rejoice in your success and encourage you to keep on in your quest. If you move to a community that is stricken by poverty and negative thinking, the odds are high that you will succumb to the "tyranny of the status quo," meaning that you will eventually become like those you surround yourself with. Solomon understood this when he said, "He that walks with wise men shall be wise, but a companion of fools shall be destroyed" (Proverbs 13:20). Pick your companions carefully. Spend time with friends who value what you value and are headed where you're headed. Look for people who have already fought the battles you are fighting and learn from them. Seek out people who have already achieved what you want to achieve and draw from their well of experience.

Course-setter 6 — Shut down negative input and shut out negative-minded people

On the surface it may sound unkind to shut out certain people, but in reality you can't help a negative person by becoming like them. When Jesus went to see the dead daughter of one of the rulers of the synagogue, He was laughed at when He said the girl was only sleeping. He first sent the "nay-sayers" out of the house and only let those who were hopeful for a positive outcome join Him in the inner chamber where the girl lay. In fact, the Bible says that Jesus did not do many miracles in His own hometown because of their negativity and unbelief. It's one thing to try to uplift someone who is in a negative frame of mind. It's quite another to choose them for a running buddy. Unless you're deliberately trying to be an influence for good in their lives, limit your contact with negative people or you may find yourself drained of your positive energy and unable to do any mighty works yourself.

Course-setter 7 — Obligate yourself to succeed

Find someone you trust who will help hold you accountable while simultaneously encouraging and uplifting you. When you tell someone else your goals and you know someone is watching, it provides an extra form of motivation to succeed. Try telling your kids, your spouse or a trusted friend. When you know people are watching, you will find yourself pushing just a little harder than you might otherwise.

Course-setter 8 — Write down your commitment to succeed and read it daily

Writing down your commitment will help you to remember your original goal when the going gets tough and the negative comments start flying. Post it on your computer screen or put it on a 3x5 card and tape it to your bathroom mirror or on your dashboard. If you put it where others will see it, you may get the extra benefit of having to explain your goal to them, which only further obligates you to succeed. That's what you really want, isn't it?

Course-setter 9 — Re-enforce your motivation with new information

Whenever possible, add to the reasons you have for wanting to succeed. Perhaps you were thinking that if you reached your goal you could take a week off for vacation. After working toward that goal, you might find something extra special you could do during that week, such as joining a mission trip or attending some special event you hadn't thought of earlier. Keep your eyes open for additional reasons to reach your goal and draw extra motivation from them.

Course-setter 10 — Stay focused

Several years ago I had a goal to set a personal sales record and hopefully win a contest in the process. The contest was for three months ending on August 31st. By August 1st, I had already achieved the sales quota for the three-month period and I still had one month to go. The way our month-ends worked, we actually had five full weeks that month to sell and my prospects looked very good at the beginning of the month. Two weeks into the month, however, things had changed and I had not gotten any sales in two weeks. As I prayed about it, the overwhelming sense I got from the Lord was to simply trust Him, so I continued.

Two more weeks passed and not only did I still not have any new sales, but every prospect I had for making a sale had evaporated into thin air. The Lord was still saying, "trust Me." Our sales quota was four units or $22,000 in revenue per month and I had never had a zero month before and I was getting nervous. Monday, Tuesday, Wednesday and Thursday all came and went in the last week of the month without any sales whatsoever.

On the eve of the last day of the sales contest where I had been hoping to shatter previous records, I was sitting on a zero month! Around midnight, one of the salesmen with whom I was competing offered to pray for me. We sat there in my office and as he prayed, something unusual happened. It was like a video clip started playing in my mind. I can't remember what he prayed, but I vividly remember the video clip. In this mental video I saw myself standing in the shallow end of a swimming pool with Jesus beside me. Jesus asked me if I wanted to be baptized, only He suggested that if I wanted, I could stay under the water for sixty seconds by supernaturally being enabled to breathe underwater. I accepted His offer, and after sixty seconds, I emerged from the water, gasping and breathing and excitedly saying, "I did it! I did it!" It was then I realized that I had held my breath—did it in my own strength—while underwater for sixty seconds. The video clip helped me understand that although I said I trusted Him, in fact I was relying on my own strength and ability to make my sales goal.

I didn't know what to do with that revelation, but the next morning I took my list of calls and instead of being uptight about the outcome, I completely left the outcome to the Lord and I just went along for the ride. The first place I called said I was lucky to catch them because they were leaving early for Labor Day, but they would listen to what I had to say. They listened and they bought a copier. The second person I called on told me the same thing, listened, and then purchased a copier. The third person I spoke with bought a copier, as did the fourth. I had hit my monthly quota in my first four calls!

My boss asked me how I was doing and I told him that I was inhaling! He probably thought I was smoking something, but I explained later what I meant.

The fifth, sixth and seventh company I called on all bought copiers. A major hospital in my territory called out of the blue and gave a purchase order for my eighth sale. The ninth, tenth, eleventh and twelfth prospects all bought copiers. At about 5:30 I came into the office with $56,000 worth of signed orders and checks, only to find there was a message from someone who wanted me to mail a brochure for our new reduction copier. I got back in my car and personally delivered it. An hour later I walked out with a $10,000 order, bringing my total to thirteen sales in a row for a total of $66,000 worth of business, which in itself was a three-month quota!

Personally, I think the feeling I felt that day must have been the same feeling that Peter felt when he obeyed Jesus and cast his net in on the other side of the boat after fishing without result all night long, and then caught the biggest haul of his career. Clearly, it wasn't about Peter's fishing skill, it was about God's intervention in the affairs of individual men. For me, I knew it wasn't about my great selling skills, my ability to trust God, or anything I did that was right. It was all about God showing Himself strong to anyone who will trust Him for the outcome.

There was never another day like that again, but there didn't need to be because I got the point. I endeavor to use my strengths and abilities to God's glory, but my hope isn't in what I can do, my hope is in Him. He is completely amazing!

Last Word

The information you have just finished reading has the potential to bring substantial increase to your life, especially in your professional sales career. For some, the contents have been a good review with the added benefit of having a Biblical foundation. For others, it's been a real revelation. For most, it's probably been a bit of both. Regardless of where you fall in the spectrum, you will get far more from this book if you deliberately and consciously apply what you've read on a daily basis.

Perhaps the best way to maximize your return on the time you invested reading this book is to make a list of prospects you want to turn into customers or customers where you want to increase your company's presence. First ask yourself, if you've been able to establish trust, respect and rapport with the client. If not, review the seven components of each principle, determine which component was not developed and consider how you can deliberately strengthen your position in each principle.

Secondly, evaluate what you know about the customer based on the seven topics discussed in the Moses Strategy for Questioning. Have you found their pain? Have you led the customer through questioning to an understanding and admission of their pain? Are you speaking with the right people? Do you know the strengths of their current system or of the competitor that's vying for the same business you are? How are you offsetting that? How can you put those strengths into perspective? How can you maximize your strengths on behalf of the customer? What kind of proofs or evidence have you offered? Have you learned how they will be evaluating potential vendors? Do you understand their buying process? When I create customized sales training programs for companies, we actually create a sales matrix where the sales person has a checklist of questions they can review to see where they stand with a potential customer at any given time. I suggest you make up your own for each customer you're working with.

Thirdly, if the principles and strategic issues are in place, then look at the motivational issues. Start with the legitimate motivational needs guarded and protected by the Ten Commandments and ask yourself if you have violated any of those ten motivational needs with any of the people involved in the buying process. Have you gone above the engineer's head without his approval? Have you tried to get a PO written while bypassing the purchasing department? Perhaps you haven't done any damage to a relationship, but you may not have won them over. Look closely at the ten motivational needs covered by the Ten Commandments and see how you can cooperate with those legitimate needs to win their willing cooperation.

The other side of the motivational coin is you. What's your attitude like? Are you being negative about this customer? Do you see little potential to make a sale because of some obstacle? I've found the biggest enemy in any selling situation is usually the sales rep. Allow yourself to see the possibilities. Always look for how things can work out instead of seeing only the reasons why they won't work out. I've found that you usually experience what you expect. Pretend for a moment that failure is not an option and ask yourself what you would do differently if you absolutely had to succeed. Then go the extra mile and do it.

Audio Coaching Program

We all need extra reinforcement of things we hold dear. Many of you like to listen to audio teaching cassettes while you drive, turning your automobile into a learning center. In addition to the book you've read, you can invest in our "Selling Among Wolves" audio coaching program. It consists of twelve, one-hour teaching tapes with matching course curriculum. It's packed full of life-changing stories and practical wisdom that you can listen to over and over again in your home or automobile. You can order that program by calling 1-800-860-7514 or by visiting our website at (www.sellingamongwolves.com).

Customized Sales Training

You may also be interested in having a fully customized sales training curriculum written and developed for your company. We accomplish this by doing an initial evaluation of your company, it's current sales process and the track record you've had for the last two or three years. This analysis may involve a field assessment with one or more of your sales reps along with candid interviews with key personnel in your organization. Based on what we learn about your company, your value proposition, your market positioning and the competitive challenges you face, we will write a complete program exclusively for your company's private use. The material we develop is based on the Biblical principles and strategies we have discussed in this book. We typically present this material in business vernacular leaving direct references to Scripture out. Essentially we teach the Biblical content without quoting the Bible verses. However some clients have asked us to be overtly Biblical in our presentation and we are only too happy to do so if asked. We will use the newly created sales training manuals in a two-day in-house training seminar. The investment for the analysis depends on the time required, but typically ranges from $2,995 to $9,995 plus travel and lodging. The investment for the training varies depending on the number of individuals attending but ranges from $895 per person to $1,195 with a five-person minimum.

Local Support Groups

If you are interested in being equipped to prosper in business so you can fend off the wolves, provide well for your family and advance God's kingdom, then you may consider joining (or leading) a local *Selling Among Wolves* support group.

Groups meet weekly all over the country for teaching, prayer, exhortation and lead exchanges. As a member you will receive a weekly coaching curriculum with practical tips to apply on the job and a prayer journal where you can record the specific business and personal needs shared by others in the group and remember them in prayer during the week.. They will be doing the same for you!

This is not meant to be a "Christian" lead exchange club, but as members we endeavor to look out for the best interests of the other members by contributing in a tangible way to their success by providing leads or sales tips for them whenever possible. It is expected that members will profit substantially from their involvement. The purpose of obtaining wealth according the Deuteronomy 8:18 is to "establish the covenant". It is hoped that each group will find a way to express that idea in a tangible way by agreeing as a local group on projects to advance the purposes of God.

How you can be involved . . .

You can join a meeting in your area as a participant. You can apply to start a local chapter in your area or you can find out about being a "strategic partner" with us as we bring the practical truths of God's Word to the business environment. For more information, please visit us at our website (www.sellingamongwolves.com) or call us at 1-800-860-7514. You may also want to make the *Selling Among Wolves* sales training programs and consulting services available to clients in your market.